# DARK PSYCHOLOGY & MANIPULATION FOR BEGINNERS

*2 Books in 1: How to Analyze People Through Manipulation Techniques and Dark Psychology Secrets*

**Marisa Leary**

Copyright 2020 by Marisa Leary. All rights reserved.

The work contained herein has been produced with the intent to provide relevant knowledge and information on the topic on the topic described in the title for entertainment purposes only. While the author has gone to every extent to furnish up to date and true information, no claims can be made as to its accuracy or validity as the author has made no claims to be an expert on this topic. Notwithstanding, the reader is asked to do their own research and consult any subject matter experts they deem necessary to ensure the quality and accuracy of the material presented herein.

This statement is legally binding as deemed by the Committee of Publishers Association and the American Bar Association for the territory of the United States. Other jurisdictions may apply their own legal statutes. Any reproduction, transmission, or copying of this material contained in this work without the express written consent of the copyright holder shall be deemed as a copyright violation as per the current legislation in force on the date of publishing and subsequent time thereafter. All additional works derived from this material may be claimed by the holder of this copyright.

The data, depictions, events, descriptions, and all other information forthwith are considered to be true, fair, and accurate unless the work is expressly described as a work of fiction. Regardless of the nature of this work, the Publisher is exempt from any responsibility of actions taken by the reader in conjunction with this work. The Publisher acknowledges that the reader acts of their own accord and releases the author and Publisher of any responsibility for the observance of tips, advice, counsel, strategies and techniques that may be offered in this volume.

# TABLE OF CONTENTS

## MANIPULATION FOR BEGINNERS
*How to Persuade and Influence People with Manipulation, Mind Control and Dark Psychology*

Introduction ............................................................................................. 3
Chapter 1 *Covering The Basics* ............................................................ 4
Chapter 2 *Persuade Or Manipulate* .................................................... 17
Chapter 3 *Techniques That Tug The Emotional Heartstrings* ............. 29
Chapter 4 *Make Them Agree If You Want Them To* .......................... 42
Chapter 5 *Under Your Spell* ................................................................ 54
Conclusion ............................................................................................. 66
Description ............................................................................................ 67

## DARK PSYCHOLOGY SECRETS
*Learn The Secrets Of The Mind And Control Your Life With Persuasion, Manipulation, And Emotional Intelligence*

Introduction ........................................................................................... 71
Chapter 1 *What Is Dark Psychology?* .................................................. 72
Chapter 2 *Characteristics Of Dark Psychology* .................................. 78
Chapter 3 *Dark Psychology Terms Explained* .................................... 86
Chapter 4 *Typical Tactics Of Dark Psychology* ................................... 94
Chapter 5 *Average People Engaging In Dark Psychology* ................ 101
Chapter 6 *The Dark Side Of Dark Psychology* .................................. 109
Chapter 7 *Dark Psychology And Social Media* ................................. 116
Chapter 8 *Deviant Behavior And Dark Psychology* .......................... 123
Chapter 9 *Making Dark Psychology Work For You* .......................... 130
Conclusion ........................................................................................... 136
Description .......................................................................................... 137

# MANIPULATION FOR BEGINNERS

*How to Persuade and Influence People with Manipulation, Mind Control and Dark Psychology*

**Marisa Leary**

© Copyright 2020 by Marisa Leary . All right reserved.

The work contained herein has been produced with the intent to provide relevant knowledge and information on the topic on the topic described in the title for entertainment purposes only. While the author has gone to every extent to furnish up to date and true information, no claims can be made as to its accuracy or validity as the author has made no claims to be an expert on this topic. Notwithstanding, the reader is asked to do their own research and consult any subject matter experts they deem necessary to ensure the quality and accuracy of the material presented herein.

This statement is legally binding as deemed by the Committee of Publishers Association and the American Bar Association for the territory of the United States. Other jurisdictions may apply their own legal statutes. Any reproduction, transmission, or copying of this material contained in this work without the express written consent of the copyright holder shall be deemed as a copyright violation as per the current legislation in force on the date of publishing and subsequent time thereafter. All additional works derived from this material may be claimed by the holder of this copyright.

The data, depictions, events, descriptions, and all other information forthwith are considered to be true, fair, and accurate unless the work is expressly described as a work of fiction. Regardless of the nature of this work, the Publisher is exempt from any responsibility of actions taken by the reader in conjunction with this work. The Publisher acknowledges that the reader acts of their own accord and releases the author and Publisher of any responsibility for the observance of tips, advice, counsel, strategies and techniques that may be offered in this volume.

# INTRODUCTION

Congratulations on purchasing *Manipulation for Beginners* and thank you for doing so.

Edward Bernays once said: *"We are governed, and our minds are molded. Our tastes are formed, and our ideas suggested. All by men that we have never met."* Bernays was the father of modern marketing, and his words sum up perfectly what manipulation involves. Bernays understood that if you wanted to get people to do what *you wanted* them to do, you had to approach them in a different way. He unstood that you cannot present someone with the facts and hope that they would see things in your favor. No, he understood that you had to use the emotional approach. He saw that if you targeted someone's emotions, the decisions they made were less rational, and thus, you could have more control and influence over the things they did.

Manipulators take advantage of other people's emotions. That is how some of the more skilled manipulators so easily wrap other people around their fingers. The most successful manipulators are always the ones you least suspect. If the manipulator does their job right, most people can go on for a long time without ever suspecting what they are up to. Is being a manipulator a bad thing? That depends. There are certain times when a little bit of manipulation could be a good thing, especially if it is done for the greater good. For example, when a parent tries to get their child to be healthy by using subtle manipulation to get them to eat their vegetables. But manipulation could also take on a darker, more sinister side. It depends entirely on what it is used for and the intention behind the manipulation.

Not all forms of manipulation are bad, and if you want to learn the art of getting people to do what you want in a subtle, non-malicious way, you have come to the right place.

There are plenty of books on this subject on the market, thanks again for choosing this one! Every effort was made to ensure it is full of as much useful information as possible, please enjoy!

# CHAPTER 1
*Covering The Basics*

The people in your life manipulate you. Maybe not all of them, but some of them certainly do. They do it so subtly that you don't even realize it is happening until you reflect on it later and say, *"Hang on, something is not quite right here."* Have you ever felt like you were being "tricked" or "forced" into doing something you didn't want to do? But you did it anyway because you felt like you had "no choice but to say yes?". *That is what mental manipulation looks like.*

## It's A Mad, Mad, Manipulative World Out There

Call it manipulation or gaslighting; manipulation is a hot topic of discussion because people are finally starting to realize just how frequently it happens. Manipulation is defined as *"controlling or influencing either a person or a situation in a clever and unscrupulous manner, or to control or play upon by means which are unfair or insidious, especially for their own advantage to serve their own purpose."* What makes manipulation such a dangerous thing is that it happens so subtly, sometimes right under our noses, and we could be completely oblivious to it. Someone else could be doing it to you, or you could be the one doing the manipulating. Either way, manipulation is considered a form of emotional and psychological abuse that can be *very harmful* to a person's wellbeing.

Manipulation. It is either happening or has happened to you. It's happening to almost everyone out there in the world today. Manipulators are people who will stop at nothing, who will do, say, and go to any lengths to get what they want. Even if it is at the expense of others. They don't think about how you feel because they're far too concerned about their own selfish needs. It's all about *"me, myself, and I"* when it comes to them. What other people want and need is irrelevant. Manipulators will keep you around as long as they have a need for you, but as soon as you no longer serve their purpose, they will cut you loose. If you were hanging off the side of a cliff with a rope, they would be the ones who cut that rope as soon as you're no longer of any use to them. Sounds brutal and harsh? That is why they call it a form of mental and emotional abuse.

A partner. A Husband. A Friend. A Wife. A Mother. A Brother. A Sister. A Colleague. A Manager. A Supervisor. It could be anyone. Anyone whom you're spending a lot of time with can manipulate you. The first sign to watch out for if you suspect manipulation is afoot is to think about this: *Do you find that you second-guess yourself quite a bit? Do you feel like you can't trust your perception of past events?* If you don't trust your own memories and question whether what you recall actually happened or not, chances are you've been gaslighted or manipulated. Manipulation is a deceptive art, and those who have mastered this art form are referred to as manipulators. Manipulative individuals exist everywhere. You could be a manipulative person yourself.

## Why Do They Call It Gaslighting?

This term is based on the 1944 film *Gaslight*. In this movie, the husband of the film's protagonist was the culprit responsible for manipulating her in such a subtle way that she believed she was losing her mind. The movie's name was based on the parts of the film where the husband was the gas lights in the upstairs floor of the flat to dim his own. When the wife brings this up, he manipulates her by trying to convince her that she is imagining it. His persistent misdirection, denial, and contradiction made the wife feel unsure of her sanity. Hence the term gaslighting, a form of emotional and psychological manipulation that is designed to make you feel unsure of your own sanity. Manipulators gaslight when they completely deny reality.

Manipulators will try to distort your thoughts and your reality. Gaslighting is when they try to gain the upper hand by making you question your reality. Manipulators will resort to this tactic when they either want to avoid responsibility, control you, manipulate you, or do all three. If they have to manipulate you to the point where you might think you're going crazy, they'll have no problems doing it through a series of frequent lies. They play games with the victim's mind by basically implying that they "feel this, think that, and thought you experienced it, but you didn't." They make you second-guess yourself by denying, twisting, and discounting everything that you say to make it seem like the victim imagined the whole thing in their mind. They could tell you you're crazy, oversensitive, forgetful, anything to make you question your sanity and your thoughts. They want you to feel like you can't be trusted to make your own decisions. Maybe you've been a victim of gaslighting quite a few times in your life too if any of these statements are starting to sound familiar.

## The Signs You're Being Gaslighted

You better believe that if someone is gaslighting you, they are doing it on purpose. They are using this manipulative tactic for a reason, and that reason is often to try and control you. They want to influence your decisions and your actions so they can try to get you to do what they want. They *always* have a hidden agenda of some sort. The worst part is, it's hard to immediately identify who might be a manipulator. On the surface, they make you believe that they're amazing. They make you yearn to be part of their crowd. They make you believe that they love you. They are charming, persuasive, and they draw you into forging some kind of a relationship with them before eventually revealing their true colors.

But underneath it all lies a sinister, underhanded character who has been toying with your emotions all along. They rely on manipulation because they want you to do what they want without saying it outright to your face. They know that if they demand point-blank that you do what they want, you're going to say no right away. That is why they prefer to choose the sneaky, underhanded approach instead.

The signs you can look out for that indicate a gaslighter might be in your presence include the following:

- You don't feel comfortable around certain people. They make you feel like you always have to have your guard up. When you know you have to be in their company, you start to feel knots in your stomach because of how much you're dreading the encounter. You might not be acutely aware that they are manipulative, but there is just something about them that makes you feel uncomfortable either before or after the encounter. Call it a sixth sense, but if your gut is telling you something is amiss, trust your gut. Even if you can't put your finger on it, if you sense something is off, it probably is.

- You feel like you are the one who has to apologize for everything when you're around them. Even if it is not your fault, they have an uncanny way of making you feel guilty when something doesn't go right. They make you worry about "letting them down" or "disappointing them." They have no qualms about making you feel bad for not helping them out, playing on your guilt, and making themselves seem like the injured party in the scenario. To avoid feeling that way, you find that you go out of your way a lot just to make them happy. Even if it is at the expense of your own happiness. Guilt is one of the manipulator's favorite tactics because it is a form of emotional manipulation. Manipulators are skilled at distorting the truth and making themselves seem like the innocent victim in any scenario.

- You find that you seem to sacrifice your happiness a lot for their sake. You put aside your needs *for their sake.* You go out of your way, above and beyond, *for their sake.* Everything is always about them. It feels like your whole life seems to revolve around them, their opinions, and their needs. They love making other people feel bad about themselves. They play on your feelings of guilt to get what they want, and when it isn't given to them, they revert back to being the victim, hoping that you'll feel guilty enough to take the action they wanted you to all along. You may be a caring, thoughtful, loving, and generous person by nature, and you don't mind doing things for others, but around these gaslighters, it feels like you're doing *too much,* and you're not comfortable with that. When you're trying to make sure everyone else is happy all the time, your own happiness ends up taking a back seat.

- You find that you're cautious about everything you say and do when you're around them. Sometimes you find that you hold back and refrain from sharing your thoughts and opinions because you're worried these might be used against you. That is a *sure sign* you're in the presence of a manipulator. If you wanted a loud and clear sign that you might be a victim of gaslighting, this is it. Your interests and feelings will never be as important as their own, and they will always look out for themselves first before anyone else. Since they usually don't like taking blame or responsibility for anything, they will go to extreme lengths to avoid it, including twisting and turning your words and throwing them back in your face.
- They make you feel guilty for talking about your problems. If they were a true friend or confidant, why would they make you feel guilty about wanting to talk about your problems? That is because they don't *want* you to talk about their problems, and they want your attention to be focused on them. By making you feel guilty, this brings the attention back to them. This puts the spotlight back on them. They love playing the victim card. When you tell them you've had a rough day at work, they'll immediately jump in with how their problem today was so much bigger. They make you pity them and *apologize* for the fact that you had a rough day at work.
- They make you feel like there is something fundamentally wrong with you. You can't quite put your finger on it, but every time you're around someone who is trying to gaslight you, there's a sense of unease. Maybe you felt confident 5-minute ago, but as soon as they came, that confidence seems to have vanished into thin air. They make you feel like you're crazy, weak, sensitive, broken, and flawed. If you feel this way, the chances are that you have been a victim of gaslighting.
- They make you feel like you need to look to them for answers because you can't trust your own judgment. If these manipulators stick around in your life long enough, you reach a point where you feel helpless when it comes to making decisions. You feel like you need to depend on them, in a way, for the answers that you seek because they have somehow convinced you that they know better. Don't be fooled, because this is what they want you to think. To get you to see things their way, manipulators will attempt to poison and distort your perception of a person or situation. Sometimes even before you have had a chance to meet the person for yourself, you find that you're already carrying around a biased opinion about them because of what the manipulator has whispered in your ear.

- They make you feel afraid of everything. Richard Nixon once said that people tend to react to fear and not to love. Manipulators love this because they use fear as one of their most powerful weapons at their disposal. They play on your fears and insecurities to get you to bend to their will by sowing the seed of fear in your mind and watering it with their comments until you go along with what they wanted all along. They love playing on your insecurities, and manipulators have an uncanny ability for sussing out situations where you may feel uncomfortable or insecure about, and they pounce on those moments, hoping to take advantage of them. If being criticized in front of others makes you feel insecure, the manipulator is going to take every opportunity they can to belittle you, undermine you, and make fun of you in the presence of others. If making mistakes makes you feel insecure, they will jump at the chance to turn even the simplest mistake and make it seem more disastrous than it really is. If you've been struggling to pinpoint why a certain someone made you feel afraid and on edge when you were around them, this could be the reason why.
- When you think about who you are now, you suddenly realize that you have become a much weaker version of yourself. Compared to the person you were before these manipulators walked into your life, you seem to have gone downhill. When you think about the person you were, you realize that you were a lot stronger before, and since they came into your life, things haven't been good. When you feel like you've become nothing but a shell of your old self, it is a sure sign that you have been (or you currently are) a victim of gaslighting.
- You realize that you have become afraid of expressing your feelings, needs, and wants when you're around them. When you're around them, you would prefer to stay quiet rather than speak your mind. That's what the gaslighter has done to you. They have manipulated you enough that you start to second-guess yourself, and you believe that your needs are not as important or valuable as the needs of others. To be more specific, they have led you to believe that *their needs* matter more than yours. They have you convinced that bending over backward to do them favors is the right way to go.

To the manipulator, pushovers are their favorite kind of people because they know that pushovers are easy targets. Manipulators will seek to gain control over you through negative reinforcement. For example, when they attempt to remove you from a negative situation and then act like they're doing you a favor. They seek to gain control over you by subtly punishing you emotionally and psychologically. This might include the silent treatment, shouting, screaming, swearing, intimidation, guilt-tripping, crying, temper tantrums, sulking, and emotional blackmail.

They might try to gain control over you through partial reinforcement too. They do this by creating a sense of fear and doubt. When the partial reinforcement is negative, they have an easier time influencing you to take a certain action you might regret later by leading you to believe you might risk losing something bigger. An example of positive partial reinforcement, on the other hand, might be in the form of encouraging the victim to carry on with a bad habit that will result in a negative outcome for the victim. A gambler might be encouraged to keep on gambling if they're a victim of partial positive reinforcement by encouraging them to believe they shouldn't pass up the opportunity to win more money.

## The Three Major Manipulative Personality Groups

Have you ever heard of the *Dark Triad Personalities?* Well, this triad is basically made up of three distinct and overlapping personalities: *Narcissism, Psychopathy, and Machiavellians.* The term dark personality is used to refer to those with a tendency for errant, sociopathic behavior that lacks empathy for others. Basically, when it comes to manipulative personality types, these are the worst of the worse. In 2002, the University of British Columbia's Delroy L. Paulhus and Kevin M. Williams conducted a study to find out just how similar these three personalities were by comparing the three dark personalities with three psychological aspects. What they discovered was that the correlation patterns were very different. Thus, what Paulhus and Williams concluded was that the dark triad personalities were distinct. Let's dive a little deeper into the difference between these personality types:

- **The Narcissist** – The Narcissists are in love with themselves. This leads them to believe they are entitled, in a way. That the whole world owes them something because they are special and they deserve special treatment. This grandiose self-image leads them to believe that they are superior to everyone else around them. When a narcissist's rosy view of themselves is challenged, they can become abusive and aggressive. In some cases where you might be romantically involved with a narcissistic manipulator, they could even resort to tactics that include sexual abuse or harassment, domestic violence or abuse, and even verbal and emotional abuse. Anything that the narcissist perceives as a threat must be immediately stomped on, in their opinion. Go against them often enough, anger them enough, and they'll resort to calling you names to demean you and drag you down. They will call you names to insult you, make you feel inferior, and undermine your opinions and credibility. Some narcissists even take pride in their behavior under the misguided notion of feeling "powerful" when they see someone else suffer at their hands. Their exaggerated levels of self-esteem make them believe they are the picture of perfection, and to themselves, they are infallible. Depending on the individual in question, the strength of the narcissistic tendencies would vary in strength, with some people having a stronger disposition towards this personality than others. Narcissism is associated with grandiosity, a distinct lack of empathy, egotism, and pride.

- **The Machiavellians** - These tend to be the more manipulative personality types. They are calculating, duplicitous, amoral, and focused on nothing but their self-interest and personal gain. The term *"Machiavellian"* actually originates from Niccolo Machiavelli, a renowned diplomat, and politician who lived in 16th century Italy. Machiavelli became notorious when his book, *The Prince*, was published in 1513. This publication was interpreted as Machiavelli's endorsement of the deceit and cunning that takes place in diplomacy. *The Prince's* reputation as a manual for tyranny seems to be well-deserved. Throughout his book, Machiavelli appears to be entirely unconcerned about morality except insofar as it is harmful or helpful when it comes to maintaining power. For example, when told to consider all atrocities necessary to seize power and commit them in a single stroke to ensure future stability. Oppressing religious minorities and attacking neighboring territories are mentioned in the book as effective ways of occupying the public. Machiavelli advises keeping up the appearance of virtues like honesty and generosity but to be ready to abandon these values as soon as your interests are threatened. The Machiavellians are perhaps the most dangerous of the lot emotionally. If you ever cross paths with a Machiavellian, you should know that they are as manipulative as they come. They'll cheat you and take great pleasure in purposely hurting you, even when there's no real rhyme or reason for them to do it. While they seldom display psychopathic tendencies, some Machiavellians have been shown to display a tendency for narcissism. Machiavellians tend to be cynical, deceptive, exploitative, and focus on their self-interest before anything else. In his book, Machiavelli famously wrote: Everyone sees what you appear to be, but very few know who you really are. Shakespeare used the word "Machiavel" to denote an amoral opportunist.
- **The Psychopaths** - These are more insensitive to the three personality groups. They lack empathy for anyone else, and they will often act without thinking. In other words, they tend to leap before they look. They are callous and impulsive, and they also happen to be the most physically dangerous personality of the

group, resorting to harmful behaviors towards others if they don't get what they want. They don't place any worth on anyone except themselves. People that have this manipulative trait could potentially be serial killers because they are predisposed to not caring about anyone except themselves. They have little to no ability to control their impulses, and this instability could then lead them to perform acts of manipulation. The brain of a psychopath may show potential damage to the frontal lobe, insula, and cerebral cortex. Since the brain's frontal lobe is the part of the brain which regulates ethics, any damage to the frontal lobe could result in possible psychopathic tendencies. Psychopaths are distinguished through their impulsive nature, selfishness, antisocial behavior, callousness, and complete lack of remorse for their actions.

What all three personalities have in common is their association with varying degrees of self-interest, questionable morals, and deception. They will deceive you more than once to try and get their way, and they're not apologetic about it when you confront them. They'll come out of nowhere and start flattering you, showering you with praise and compliment right before casually slipping in favor that they need you to do. They will display a complete lack of remorse and morals for their actions. They will make remarks against you or others that are both callous, derisive, and thoughtless. If they're narcissistic, they'll boast and brag to no end, wanting everyone around them to know just how wonderful they are. They find it difficult to accept that someone could be better at them. When they perceive such individuals to be in their midst, they will work hard at tearing them down or holding them back, just so they can be the ones ahead of the pack once more. They will belittle the accomplishments of others, and they will have a jaded view or perception of the world.

Psychopathy and narcissism have a closer link to each other than narcissism. Quite possibly because narcissism is the only personality trait out of the three that stems from insecurity, all three personalities, however, tend to be morally disengaged. This allows them to behave unethically and not feel any remorse over their actions. All three members of the dark triad group share similar behavior characteristics when they are in various social settings. For example, at work, you might find one of these dark personalities in the form of an entitled boss or a colleague who is not shy about using underhanded tactics to weasel their way to the top. They might be the ones who can't seem to make any genuine connections with the people around them. They have a tendency towards egoism, where they were preoccupied with their own achievements. If they had to accomplish those achievements at the expense of others, they would. They also happen to be psychologically entitled, believing that they were superior to everyone else and therefore entitled to get anything that they wanted. They are preoccupied with their own self-interest and desire to boost either their financial or social status. If they had narcissistic tendencies, they would brag about their own superiority.

All three of the dark personalities behave impulsively at times because they lack empathy and self-control. Some can be more sadistic than others, deriving pleasure from mentally or physically inflicting harm on another. What makes them unpleasant to be around is their spiteful tendencies, and how they were willing to retaliate or harm others even if they had to hurt themselves in the process. It's not uncommon for these manipulative characters to try and play the "victim" card in nearly every situation to gain sympathy, and will do whatever it takes to make you feel sorry for them. Besides their displays of social entitlement, all three of the dark personalities have several different ways of interacting with the people around them. Psychopaths and Machiavellians, for example, tend to be cynical and morally suspicious of others. Narcissists, on the other hand, have a skewed sense of self. They think of themselves as better leaders and believe that they are more empathetic than they really are.

The narcissists are also prone to something called *The Triangulation Dynamic*. This dynamic is created when the narcissist starts to put two people against each other, causing a rift between them so deep that both sides believe the problem lies with the other instead of the narcissist. A narcissistic parent could pit two children against each other. A narcissistic man would pit two women against each other and vice versa. It is an extremely effective technique, and it works well as a distraction, and the narcissists love it because this is what they wanted from the beginning. It keeps the blame off them, while simultaneously feeding into their ego of being "desired" when there are two people fighting for their affections. They take pleasure in the notion of being "fought over," and they take even more pleasure from knowing that they have that kind of control or influence over others. Narcissists crave attention, thanks to their inflated sense of self. They need it to feed into their egos and belief about their own self-importance.

## Sociopaths versus Psychopaths

It's easy to confuse between the two if you're not extensively familiar with what these personality traits entail. Both seem to be almost similar, but why is one listed as a dark personality trait and not the other? Sociopaths and psychopaths are both parts of the antisocial personality disorder group, and both share a lack of empathy and moral judgment. Some experts believe that sociopathy and psychopathy tend to be one and the same and group them together, while others would argue that there are significant differences between the two disorders. The outward behavior displayed by sociopaths and psychopaths can be as different as night and day. But what distinguishes between the two personalities is that psychopaths are pathological liars (hence the manipulation). They don't mind lying through their teeth if it means they are going to get what they want. Do they feel guilty about it? Not even a little bit. They are willing to lie and spin any story they can if it is going to benefit their agenda at the end of the day. Psychopaths also tend to be fearless, and they have become so good at mimicking behaviors you can't tell you're dealing with a psychopath right away.

The first impression you get of a psychopath could be negative right away since they actually want to appear intimidating. Perhaps what makes them extremely dangerous is their uncanny ability to mimic the people around them so well. No story illustrates this better than the story of Gary Ridgeway, a perfect example of a psychopath's immense lying skills and an inability to feel empathy and form emotional attachments. Between 1982 and 2001, Ridgeway murdered at least 49 women in Washington, most of his victims being prostitutes or young women who ran away. After he killed them, he would often return to his dumping ground, where he would then have sex with the corpses. Some of the bodies were dumped in the Green River, which earned Ridgeway the name Green River Killer. While he committed some of these horrible crimes, he was married to this third wife at the time. Although he targeted prostitutes because he hated them, he loved his wife and had a good relationship with her. In an interview with his wife after Ridgeway went to prison, she still had difficulty coming to terms with the fact that her husband was a serial killer, even going so far as to describe their life together as "loving and content."

It can sometimes take a long time before a psychopath's true colors are revealed. A psychopath may sometimes resort to another approach by getting you to feel sorry for them. They shift the focus of your attention towards them, their needs, and their so-called "misfortunes." They'll regale you with tales that make you feel sorry for them and feel bad enough for them to shower all your time, and attention is completely devoted to making them "feel better." They will go to any lengths to get the attention they seek, even if they must make up some stories along the way. As we can see from the Ridgeway story, psychopaths are capable of hurting others without any guilt or remorse. This makes psychopathy one of the most dangerous forms of all antisocial behavior since psychopaths can dissociate emotionally from their actions, even if those actions are horrifically terrible. They might try to compensate for this tendency by being skilled actors, charming and persuasive, capable of faking emotions that
they cannot feel. They can play whatever role is required of them to win the trust and manipulate others. They create a veneer of social respectability to hide their dark side and any sinister behavior resulting from it.

A key trait that distinguishes sociopaths is that they tend to have a conscience, albeit a weak one. But it is there, nonetheless. They can be self-centered, but sociopaths do care for others. Psychopaths don't care who they have to hurt to get their way. Sociopaths are not that great at hiding their behavior, which explains why they're not listed in the dark triad manipulative personality group. Manipulators have to be skilled at hiding their agenda, or everyone is going to know what they are up to and stay away from them.

For a sociopath, their indulgence and lack of empathy are pretty obvious and noticeable for those who pay attention to the body language cues. A sociopath is more impulsive, irresponsible, tend to to "live on the fringes of society" according to psychologist Scott Bonn, and they can't settle in one place or hold a job for long If they can find legitimate work for what they need, they may resort to shady activity such as lying, cheating, and stealing from people along the way. Charles Ponzi is one example of a sociopath. Ponzi famously said he "supposedly" immigrated to American with only $2.50 in his pocket in cash and $1 million in hopes and dreams. After he arrived in Boston, he spent several years working odd jobs and led a life of lies that was focused on tricking people into investing in sham corporations. One example is his International Reply Coupon Scheme. He used money from investors to pay other investors. This became the infamous *The Ponzi Scheme,* and it is still used as an example today of what a sociopath is capable of.

## Who Are They?

No one likes being manipulated. But there are some people out there who deserve an award for how good they are at the art of deception. Sometimes, their victims could go for years without ever realizing that they are being manipulated, like the example of Gary Ridgeway. Although skilled at hiding their true colors, if you know what to look out for, you can spot a manipulator before they have time to do too much damage. Here are some signs to watch out for that alert you to their presence:

- **Attention-Seekers** - Demanding constant attention from you is one of the many typical behaviors of a manipulator. They give off the impression that they are weak, "helpless," and always in need of your help. However, this approach puts them in a powerful positive in the lives of whom they have come to depend on. By acting helpless, they stroke the ego of the people that they depend on, which allows the manipulators to gain a sense of control, but they can quickly become nasty if someone were to resist their request for help or a favor. They won't respect your space and will continually demand attention, even when you have made it obvious that their request is going to inconvenience you.

- **Emotional Blackmail** - They have an uncanny ability to make you feel guilty without actually demanding outright that you do what they want. This tactic is known as emotional blackmail. When you're faced with this situation, they put you in a tough spot, and it makes you feel like you're being forced to do things against your will. They bank on the fact that you're going to feel guilty not being a good friend or partner to them, and they use the emotional blackmail approach to fulfill their own agendas.
- **Indirect Communicator** - They're always sneaky, and they will have something up their sleeves all the time. They will rarely tell you what they are thinking because they want to avoid being caught out. It is important that nothing tarnishes their "good person" image, and they would rather talk about you behind your back than to your face.
- **The "Poor Victim"** – This is a classic and favorite manipulative tactic. In almost every situation, these manipulators will always feel sorry for themselves, and they want others to feel sorry for them too. They seek out sympathy, and they don't mind turning people against each other in order to do it. The thing about these manipulators is they will be the ones who start the fight, yet will end up twisting and turning the entire situation around so that they end up the "victim." When it comes to playing the victim, the manipulator is an expert at seeming small and defenseless, even when nothing could be further from the truth. Don't be fooled by their fake innocence.
- **The All or Nothing Ultimatum** - to get you to go along with what they want, they force you into a corner by giving you an ultimatum that often leaves you no choice but to side with them. Someone who genuinely loved you or cared about you would never make you resort to such a thing. They would never put pressure on you to give up something they know that you loved, or that meant a lot to you. If the manipulator in your relationship doesn't like your friends, they could make you choose between being with them or giving up your friendship. They make you feel pressured into choosing them by instilling the fear that you might lose them if you don't. This type of manipulation can even occur in friendships, where your manipulative friend who might be jealous of a new friendship that you formed makes you choose one or the other.
- **Their Problems Matter More** - Your problems will always be trivial compared to theirs. They will always attempt to minimize your problems by comparing it to theirs. Combined with their talent for playing the victim, they can quickly make you feel guilty for bringing up your issues, even when you had a valid reason to do so. They love making other people feel bad about themselves.

They play on your feelings of guilt to get what they want, and when it isn't given to them, they revert back to being the victim hoping that you'll be guilty enough to take the action they wanted you to all along.

# CHAPTER 2
## *Persuade Or Manipulate*

In many circumstances, you'll find that persuasion is a handy trick that will prove useful to you. Being a persuasive person is one of the most useful skill sets you can master. You could use it to coax your boss into giving you the raise you know you deserve, persuade a client to seal the deal, persuade a friend to try out that new restaurant you know they will love, getting your partner or friends to see your point of view, there is so much you could accomplish when you learn how to become just a little more persuasive. But hold on, isn't persuasion almost the same thing as manipulation?

Defining and Understanding Persuasion

Before we can understand the differences that separate manipulation from persuasion, we need to understand what persuasion means. We persuade people around us all the time, and we are clearly doing it with our own self-interest in mind. Persuasion, on its own, is not evil. It is simply a means by which we interact with the people around us. You persuade a friend to meet up with you after work for a drink because you need someone to talk to, even when you know that friend may be tired after a long day at the office. You persuade your teammates to with your approach on a project at work because you know your way is the more efficient one.

Every day, we speak. We utter thousands of words, but do we ever give those words much thought? There is a quote that goes: *Handle them carefully, for words are more powerful than atom bombs*. When words are used and spoken in the right way, they can literally get anyone to do anything that you want them to. Words have the power to change the human mind. Words influence the way we think, how we interpret the information that we receive, and words have an impact on the way we formulate and come to a decision. The way that you choose to present information could sometimes be the difference between gaining a new friend and turning them away completely. Two people who could be similar in every way could have very different results when they try to achieve success. The one who achieves success is often the one who knows how to make every word count. The one who happens to be *more persuasive*.

When you speak the right combination of words, it speaks directly to a person's subconscious. When used correctly, this technique can be used to triumph over lies. By nature, human beings are a curious species. We are often in search of answers and truths. We want to know why things work the way they do, and we have always been in search of answers for as long as we can remember. We ask questions, we discuss, we argue, we explore philosophy, science, even art just to get the answers we desire.

When your view conflicts with that of someone else's, we fall into a game of persuasion, bouncing ideas and facts back and forth as each party tries to convince the other that they are right. The subconscious mind is only able to process yes and no answers, and it tends to make decisions quickly using a few key phrases. That is why the right combination of words and speaks in the way the subconscious mind works can make you instantly more influential and persuasive.

Aristotle wrote a book called *Rhetoric*. In his book, he laid out what he believed to be the three foundations for the art of persuasion, and all three of these foundations distinctly show why persuasion is *not the same thing* as manipulation. In the first foundation, Aristotle believed that persuasion had an element of credibility. He believed that we tend to be more easily persuaded if we believe the person to be trustworthy. Aristotle claimed that a trustworthy person should have three qualities about them, and these were good morals, good sense, and goodwill. When we believe that someone has good moral character when we trust that they will do the right thing, we believe that a person has goodwill when we believe that they have no ulterior motive. A person comes across as having good sense when we believe that we can trust their judgment, and believe that they are rational thinkers who are capable of staying calm and collected.

The second foundation was emotion. When making a decision, we would like to think that people, in general, use all the information available to them to make an informed, unbiased decision. The reality, though, is not the case. People are emotional, and they make decisions primarily based on emotions most of the time. Depending on how we feel at the time, we may be more or less inclined to agree with the other party if we're in the right emotional state at the time of discussion. One way to be as persuasive as you can be is by effectively tapping into their emotions. It is often the way that you make someone feel that leaves the strongest impression. They may forget what you've said, but they'll never forget the way you made them feel. The third foundation, according to Aristotle, was logic. People are more easily convinced when the logic is both strong and easy to follow. To be more persuasive, you have to put forth a sound logical argument. A conclusion is made based on the premises of your argument. These are definitely not traits you would find if manipulation was present.

## But Is Persuasion *Manipulative?*

Yes, it sure is. But the thing is, *persuasion is okay.* Yes, it is manipulative, but it's not the far end of the manipulation spectrum where it's all bad news. Persuasion is the *good kind* of manipulation. While manipulation is not going to win you any friends, persuasion can. It can turn your prospective customers into long-term clients. It can turn fans into super fans. Persuasion skills that are used for the right reason can bring about a lot of benefits. Unlike manipulation, where the only person getting something out of it is the one who is doing all the manipulating. A master persuader is someone who knows how to turn a "no" into a "yes," and how to do it without having to lie, cheat, or backstab anybody. But persuasion that is overused can quickly spill over into manipulative territory, so we need to be a little careful right there. There's a very fine, sometimes blurry line that separates the two, and it is when we understand the very definition of what these two terms mean can we begin to distinguish when we may be crossing the line from persuasion and manipulation.

Think of manipulation and persuasion as close relatives, if you will. The easiest way to know if you're crossing over into manipulative territory is when you try to get the other person to do something that is of interest *to you*. You don't really care if it is an inconvenience to them or if it's obvious they don't want to do it. All you care about is your own interest, and you want it done no matter who you have to push to do it in the 4th century BC. Aristotle, the father of persuasion, found himself opposing a group of teachers who were referred to as the Sophists. These Sophists were infamous for their rhetorical teachings, and Aristotle found himself butting heads with these groups of individuals over the fact that the Sophists did not seem to care about truth at all, and they were willing to promote just about any idea for a price. Aristotle firmly believed that the Sophists were engaging in manipulative behavior since there was an apparent intention to deceive others. If there is a genuine desire to help another, and that is the only reason why you may be forcing someone to do something they don't want to do, that could be considered an acceptable form of manipulation.

When it's persuasion, it is usually in the interest of both parties. Everyone hopefully gets to benefit from persuasion and not just you alone. Persuasion still gives people the freedom to choose between whether they want to reject or accept the idea which is being presented to them. Yes, you are trying to move them to side with your point of view, but you're not bullying, begging, or pushing them to do it. Persuasion is trying to convince others by carefully framing your arguments, and by presenting supporting evidence while leaving it up to them to make the final decision on where they stand. It is a *mild form* of manipulation if you really need to compare. Another thing about persuasion is that it is *only effective when you take the time to get to know the other person*. What motivates them? What drives them? What pains them? The most effective and persuasive people out there are the ones who know their audience. When they know who their target audience is, they tailor their messages to fit the needs of the audience. They know that if they want to gently sway their audience and convince them to change their minds, they need to speak to their hearts, not their heads.

If you don't know who your audience is, you cannot persuade them. If you don't know who your audience is, *but* you still try to get them to do what you want, you're manipulating. If your intention is not in the best interest of someone else, then what you are doing is being manipulative. This is quite difficult to do since we are naturally programmed to think about ourselves and our needs first before we think about anyone else's needs. Unfortunately, this is something which happens far too often, and if you suspect you could be on the receiving end of this behavior, take a good look at whether the outcome is benefiting you, or just the manipulator alone. Manipulators don't usually have the best intentions because they don't see others as equal to them. The only thing they care about is their agenda, and everything else comes secondary.

People are not resistant to change. We're adaptable as a species. We're not resistant to change, but we do resist *being changed*. We resist when we think we are being forced to go along with someone else's agenda. We resist when we think someone else is trying to control us. Manipulators may be successful at forcing people to get what they want, but it comes at a price. They never build genuine relationships once people realize what they are up to. Nobody likes being told they are wrong. Nobody likes having their beliefs and opinions rebuked, and all its flaws laid out in detail. When someone tries to prove you wrong, most people would become defensive and attempt to walk away, hoping to never see you again. Persuasion is not about winning or proving that you know better. If you take this approach, you're never going to achieve any kind of success, even if you happen to be right.

If you want to become a more persuasive person, you need to focus on using your skills for good. Focus on what you can do to make someone else's life a little bit better or a little bit easier. Think about what you can do for them that might brighten their day. Persuasion could be a good thing because, at its very core, it is the pursuit of the truth. Through the right amount of persuasion, change for the better can take place. A lot of the good work that gets done today would not be possible without persuasion in play. When used in the right way, persuasion will never be as damaging or detrimental as manipulation is. For example, persuasive messages that are delivered in the form of campaigns that encourage us to quit smoking or donate blood to help save lives. The right kind of persuasion can be responsible for uniting nations and forging peace agreements. Charities and fundraising organizations rely on persuasion to help them raise awareness and drive the donations that they need to continue with their charitable work. Parents rely on persuasion to teach their children about safe and stranger danger. If you want to be persuasive, you need to think about what the nature of your intention is. Do you think about the other person and how they could benefit from it too? Or are you only thinking about yourself and nothing else? Whether you're persuading or manipulating, it all boils down to your intention.

# Psychology Tricks Commonly Used to Persuade Anyone

When you want to use it, it can come in handy if you know a few psychological tricks that could help you easily persuade others to go along with what you want, especially when you're faced with someone who has strong opinions and can be difficult to convince. Persuasion is like a healthy debate. You're presenting someone with the reasons why they should agree with you and come over to your side. There's no sneakiness and no blatant deception at play. You're simply presenting the facts and justifying them with supporting evidence while leaving the rest up to the listener to draw their own conclusions.

This is why certain psychological tricks work so well in the game of persuasion. You're simply telling them the facts, and then leaving the final decision up to them, hoping that you have convinced them enough to make the right choice at the end of the day. The power of *choice* is the one that makes the biggest difference of all. With persuasion, you're not forcing someone to take action. There's no *"do this or else"* approach that makes them feel like they have no choice but to do what you ask. Persuasion is situational. The techniques that work well in one context might not be as effective in another. To pull it off, you're going to have to rely on a multitude of communication skills. To appear more persuasive and less manipulative, you could employ the following tactics:

- **Explaining Why You're Making the Request** - Although technically we don't owe anyone an explanation for why we want to do something, there are moments when explaining why you're making a request could help your cause. For example, when you're waiting in a long line at the supermarket but you're in a rush because you have another appointment to get to. Explaining your reasons for getting ahead of everyone else in the queue might make them more willing to let you do it if they knew you had a valid reason. When your reason is compelling enough, people are a lot more likely to listen to your point of view. Perhaps even agree with you if they can empathize and put themselves in your shoes. The bigger your request, the more compelling your reason should be.
- **Be Polite** - Politeness is a quality that gets overlooked so many times. When was the last time you thought about the importance of being polite? There are only two words in the English language that can work magic when you're trying to persuade the people around you. Those words are *please* and *thank you*. People are more open to requests than they are to instructions. If you demonstrate politeness with your requests every step of the way, you are 100% more likely to get other people to say yes to you. Nobody likes to feel like they are forced to do something. They

don't like feeling like they had no choice in the matter. A simple please and thank you alongside your requests, combined with a genuine smile, can work wonders.
- **Be Honest When You're Presenting Your Facts** - Since persuasion is not about spinning lies in the hopes of pulling the wool over someone else's eyes, you're going to be focusing on facts when you try to influence others. You need to present *both* sides of the coin, good and bad, happy and sad. This approach works well because it respects the fact that your audience knows there are two sides to every viewpoint. The next time you're listening to a speech by an influential individual, notice how they present an opposing viewpoint or two instead of just sticking solely to why their argument is right. They know audiences are more likely to be persuaded when you address their concerns and provide solutions to ease their worries. What you're presenting may be focusing on the benefits, but at the same time, by presenting both points of view, you're not disregarding the other side of the story, and your audience is going to appreciate this. Persuasive people use this approach all the time, they talk about the benefits of their argument, acknowledge the potential negative outcomes that could come as a result of their approach, and then once more discuss how beneficial their idea can be in mitigating the problems.
- **Listen Actively** - The most effectively persuasive people you will ever meet are the ones who are active listeners. Listening is a very important part of becoming a more persuasive person. You see, when you're trying to persuade someone, you're trying to get them to listen to your ideas or get their consent. To get them to *accept* your requests, however, the ability to listen is going to serve you well. When you listen actively, it helps you understand the person that you are trying to persuade. This is where you find out what worries, reservations, or objections they might have to your request or proposal. When you know what might be holding them back, you can begin working on phrasing or wording your requests in such a way that they become more appealing. In the game of persuasion, listening is going to trump talking every single time.
- **Compliment Them** - When it comes to the art of persuasion, compliments can go a long way toward helping your cause. People love to be complimented, even if they won't admit it out loud to themselves. The minute you offer someone a genuine compliment, they immediately become open and receptive to what you have to say. That is the opening you've been waiting for to slowly wedge your request in the door. A compliment can be extremely effective in changing someone's preconceived notions

about you. But this only works if the compliment is sincere. It's not going to work if they feel like you are trying too hard. For this tactic to work, you need to make sure that your compliments are both subtle and honest at the same time. An insincere compliment can quickly backfire and have the opposite effect of what you hoped it would do.

- **Using Speech That Is Fluid** - When you're trying to persuade, confidence is the key to winning. When your sentences are colored with hesitant words, like *hmm, ummm, like, I mean,* for example, it gives the impression that you're not as confident. It makes the listener feel as though you're not sure what you're talking about. When speech is fluid, it gives the impression of being confident and self-assured. The more confident you appear to be in your speech, the easier it is going to be for you to persuade others.
- **Faster Speech** - Another persuasive trick is to talk at a faster rate when you're trying to convince someone of what you want. When you're speaking quickly, the person that you're speaking too doesn't have enough time to properly process every single piece of information you're giving them. They might not be able to soak in everything that you're saying to them, and this is an opportunity for you to quickly swing things in your favor. When they don't have enough time to process all the information, they don't have enough time to pick apart your points. Persuasive people make it a point to know who their audience is, and if they know they're going to be in the presence of those who are likely to disagree with them, they adjust the rate of their speech and talk faster. They do the opposite when they know the crowd they're addressing is more likely to agree with what they're saying. When you talk faster and fluidly, it gives the appearance of confidence too. People will be more inclined to listen to what you have to say when you give the appearance that you confidently know what you are talking about.
- **Repeat Their Words** - Another psychologically persuasive trick is to repeat the words that the other person is saying to you. Not everything, of course, you don't want to give the impression of being a copycat or a parrot, mimicking everything that they say. The purpose of repeating some of the things they say to you gives them the impression that you're listening. That you are acknowledging that their opinions matter enough for you to take them seriously. This makes them happy, and when they are happy, they're easily persuaded. Making anyone that you're talking to happy by giving the impression you're paying attention to them will help establish a bond between the two of you, even if you have just met. That rapport will open their minds to the

requests or favors you need to ask of them. Psychologists have been known to use this tactic a lot when communicating with their patients to get them to relax. Be careful not to overuse this tactic, though. You don't want to come across as being weird.

- **Nod Along** - Another quick trick to get people to think you're paying attention to them is to nod along when they're talking. The best persuaders know what an effective technique nodding can be. Robert Cialdini, author of *Influence: The Psychology of Persuasion*, says feeling similar to someone is one of the six most powerful factors in the art of persuasion. Sharing something in common or feeling similar puts two people in sync, which then allows for the pacing and leading of conversation. Two people who are in sync often mirror each other, moving in the same way or even thinking the same thoughts sometimes. Nodding occasionally lets them know that you're affirming the things that they say. It makes them feel supported, and without even realizing it, they'll find themselves being open and receptive to what you have to say in return. Reaffirming nods from you make the other person subconsciously more accommodating and agreeable too.

- **Invest in Getting to Know Them** - If you only approach them whenever you need something, eventually, the person is not going to be very receptive to your requests anymore. They'll think that the only time you ever truly make an effort or come and talk to them is when you want something. That is never a good impression. Successful persuasion calls for balance. When you take, you must be willing to give back in return. You need to be willing to invest the time and energy, developing a rapport with them instead of flat out trying to shove your request in their face right away. You need to demonstrate respect for what they say and never belittle them, even if you happen to disagree with their ideas. You need to get them to *trust* you enough to listen to you with an open mind. One of the best techniques to subtly encourage trust is to mirror them. Use the same tone of voice, the same mannerisms, and the same gestures that they use. The mirror technique inspires confidence when you use the same language that they are using. It makes them feel like you really understand them, and they will eventually begin to trust you. Meet them on their level and show that you're willing to listen, not just make demands all the time.

- **Be Humble, Be Kind** - As keen as you may be to persuade someone to go along with what you want, always maintain honesty and never fudge the truth just to get what you want. That's crossing the line to manipulation and deception when you do that. Simple acts of kindness will go a long way, and they will be remembered when the time comes, and you happen to need to persuade someone to help you out. It also goes a long way towards building trust by showing that you genuinely care about the way that they feel and that you want them to be happy with the agreed-upon outcome. Always be honest and transparent in your attempts to persuade others. Once they find out that they can't trust you, or that you have misled them in any way, you'll find it hard to convince anyone ever again when the bond of trust has been broken. Each time you show gratitude towards others, express your thanks, treat them with respect, and do favors or lend a helping hand to those who happen to need it most, you win their trust.

- **Do Them A Favor** - When you do someone a favor, most of the time, they will feel obligated to return the favor. Unless they happen to be manipulators who only care about themselves. The best kind of favors are the unexpected ones, and if you do something genuinely nice for someone else, they'll return the favor when the time comes. That time is when you need to persuade them to do something for you. The give and take dynamic is one of the most powerful persuasive techniques. Sometimes you don't even have to say a lot. All you have to do is be nice and promote a relationship based on give and take. When you are nice to others, they'll do the same for you. That way, you're less likely to be rejected when it is time to put forth your requests.
- **Offer A Beverage** - If you're trying to persuade someone over coffee, lunch, dinner, breakfast, or any occasion where food and drink might be present, a subtle persuasive technique you could use is to offer that person a drink. Even better if it is a warm drink like coffee or tea. Offering someone a warm drink psychologically projects feelings of warmth toward you, the person who offered them the beverage. This makes them feel like you are someone who is likable and welcoming.
- **Employ the Contracts Technique** - A method that is used in bargaining, the contrast technique is when you make a demand that is higher than what you actually want. Gradually, you "bargain down" to what you wanted, and it tricks the other person into thinking they're getting a better deal. The huge contrast between the first demand and the last demand is the winning formula. In their minds, the lower offer is a lot more ideal and doable than the first one, which means they will be more inclined to say yes to you.
- **Let Them Think You Can Walk A Mile in Their Shoes** - The secret to successful persuasion is by focusing on how or what you can do to be helpful to other people. Your ability to step into

their world, think what they think, feel what they feel, and be empathetic, that's going to be the key to transforming the relationships that you start to form with them. Most people tend to focus on how they persuade someone else enough to get them to do what they want, when instead what they should be focusing on is how they can be helpful. See the situation from their point of view. If the roles were reversed, what would you need to hear from them in order to convince you? When you try to convince them from an angle that highlights how beneficial it is going to be in resolving a problem or issue that they may be having, or even if it addresses a certain need that they want, it becomes much easier to get them to go along with your agenda. People want to see what's in it for them, and when you can show them the ways they will benefit from your approach, they'll be more than happy to hop over to your side without question.

- **Timing Is Everything** - If you play your cards right and time it well, you can work the situation in your favor. A little interesting fact about people is that they tend to be a lot more agreeable when they are mentally tired. If you know your request might not be well received right away, a little trick you could use is to try and persuade them after they have done something that demanded a lot of mental energy. Even if you can't get them to respond right away, they will at least be willing to listen to your demands. This technique will depend heavily on the person in question, and it's not always going to work. But it is something to keep in mind in your endeavor to be more persuasive. It never hurts to try.

## Key Phrases to Winning Them Over

With a few key phrases, you can quickly become a more persuasive person *without* the need to be overly manipulative. You will find it a lot easier to get people to agree with you or go along with what you want in general. Words can be a powerful force of good when used for the right reasons, but on the other end of the spectrum, it can be used not only to control another but to inflict great harm and pain. The phrase the pen is mightier than the sword stems from the very real fact that words can cause a great deal of pain and leave scars so deep they might never fully recover. But if you used your words wisely, you could become an immensely powerful, influential person without having to force anyone to do your bidding.

What are these power phrases? These are by far the best that you can start with:

- **I'm Not Sure If It's for You** - Add the word "but" at the end of that sentence, and it will allow you to introduce an idea easily and in a clever, unsuspecting manner. The other person is not going to realize what you're doing at all because they will be too preoccupied, thinking about what you just said. When you say something like, *"I'm not sure if it's for you, BUT I thought it would be a good idea,"* it instantly tells their subconscious that there is no pressure. By implying that they might not be interested from the start, it has the opposite effect. After all, we're known for wanting what we cannot have. Tell them they might not be interested in something, and they will instantly become a lot more interested.

- **Open-Minded** - This is going to work very similarly to the power phrase above. All you need to do is add this word *before* what you want to present. For example, if you were trying to get your friend to loan you their car for the weekend, phrasing your statement with the word open-minded, immediately increases your chances of them saying yes. *"How open-minded would you be about letting me borrow your car this weekend? I really need one, and mine is in the workshop."* The reason this simple word is going to work so well is that people like to think of themselves as open-minded. When you insert this word into your request, their subconscious brain tells them that going against your request is going to make them seem like they are not open-minded at all. This makes it difficult for them to say no since most people would prefer to preserve a good image of themselves.
- **What Do You Know** - This combination of words is like the final knockout punch you deliver to win any argument or discussion. Especially if you're dealing with someone who is stubbornly refusing to listen to reason because they think that they know everything already. When two people are in a discussion or argument, each person has their own opinion. This opinion is usually based on a foundation of knowledge that they have about a certain topic. Some people like to think that they know everything, and they love to appear superior. The *"what do you know"* phrase is a confident way of calling them out. Indirectly put them on the spot without being too obvious by challenging their knowledge about the subject. It can make them doubt their own opinion, and that is when you swoop in with the winning punch.
- **How Would You Feel** - This next winning combination of words can get anyone to do anything you want by playing on their emotions. Not to the point of manipulation, but just a little bit. *How would you feel if, by this time next week, you still couldn't persuade your client to close the deal with you?* How did that sentence make you feel? Chances are, that sentence probably stirred some emotions in you. A feeling of loss, almost as if you would be losing out on something if you didn't get the deal. Every

decision that we make is a decision that moves us in two directions. Pain or pleasure. This is what every decision is based on, and that is why this winning combination of words is going to work extremely well. We are all motivated to move away from anything that might cause pain. Phrase your statement right, and you will have people eating out of the palm of your hand if they believe by doing so, they are moving away from pain.

- **Just Imagine** - If someone can't imagine themselves doing something in the real world, they're not likely to do it. For example, before a woman agrees to go out with you, she must be able to picture what the two of you would look like in her head. Even men do the same thing. If either the man or woman can't see themselves with each other, they're not likely to say yes. When a wealthy person walks into a dealership to buy a Lamborghini, they don't need to think about the purchase. They're already decided on the car because they have pictured themselves driving it in their minds. By using the words *just imagine,* you can plant an image in a person's mind that gets them thinking about what it would be like if they were to go along with your request.

The way that you say these words matters as much as the words themselves. You need to be over-confident when you're using these power phrases, even if you might not be feeling all that confident yourself. The more confident you are, the greater your chances of persuading other people to sway over to your side of the fence. Your words are powerful, and you could be using them to get what you want out of life if you know how to use them correctly. Don't forget about your body language too. No one is going to be convinced in your idea if your shoulders are hunched, and you're slouched the entire time. Stand up straight with your shoulders back, maintaining good posture, and project an air of confidence. Just imagine if you did that? You would have no problems winning anyone over.

# CHAPTER 3
## Techniques That Tug The Emotional Heartstrings

Emotional manipulators. What is it about them that makes them so dangerous? Well, for one thing, when an emotional manipulator has their sights set on you, they are not going to stop until they have you wrapped around their finger. Their mission is to use stealth to control you and to get away with it for as long as they possibly can. The trouble with emotional manipulators is that they can be so incredibly likable. They make you fall in love with them and crave their attention to the point that we are willing to follow them with blind ignorance. Even when the signs are there, we don't want to see it because it's a hard pill to swallow. How could someone so likable be manipulating us? Are they using us for their hidden agenda? The sad truth is, they can and they will.

## How Emotional Manipulators Sink Their Claws Into Their Victims

Emotional manipulators are known for playing the guilt card. Guilt can be a very powerful, emotional driver. It never feels good to feel guilty, and the manipulator is going to bank on the fact that you want to avoid this emotion. They have no qualms about making you feel bad for not helping them out, playing on your guilt, and making themselves seem like the injured party in the scenario. This is a cunning way of getting you to agree to their agenda without seeming suspicious. This sly individual will subtly play on your emotions by making you feel as though you were the selfish one, the one who didn't "care" enough to be there for the manipulator when they needed it. They would even stoop so low as to make you feel bad for prioritizing your needs over theirs. Emotions are powerful, and guilt is one of the most powerful ones that we possess. Guilt can make you do things you don't want to do, just to avoid feeling bad about the fact that you had to say no to someone or turn them down. To make this tactic work, the emotional manipulator must distort the truth and make themselves seem like the innocent victim in any scenario. They love poking on your weak spots, and in some twisted way, they delight in your misery.

They will guilt you, they will blame you, and they will shame you. They act like a martyr, subtly implying guilt by pointing out how everything they did was "for your benefit" or "because of you." Some manipulators love applying this tactic to make you feel bad enough. In doing so, they end up doing what the manipulator wanted all along. They love making other people feel bad about themselves. They play on your feelings of guilt to get what they want, and when it isn't given to them, they revert back to being the victim, hoping that you'll feel guilty enough to take the action they wanted you to all along. Guilt is the emotions that they use against you, and guilt is the emotion that they use to sink their claws into you.

## Emotional Manipulation Is Emotional Abuse

There is no justifying why you would manipulate someone emotionally. Emotional manipulation, like other forms of manipulation, can be classified as abusive because of the scars and the trauma they leave behind on the victim. Emotional manipulation is a lot more common than we realize. Sometimes, this form of manipulation takes place even among those who are not manipulative by nature. It happens sometimes. We all need to manipulate for one reason or another. We don't notice because we're not paying attention. We blow things off, we let it slide because we don't want to make a big deal out of it. Emotional abuse is not as obvious as other forms of manipulation, but it is perhaps more dangerous because it doesn't get talked about enough. People don't reach out for help, and they don't know how to react or respond when they realize they have been a victim of emotional abuse.

Emotional abuse is about two things: *Power and control.* The person who is the abuser (the manipulator) will always be the one who tries to gain more power and control over everyone else. Emotional manipulation is damaging. Mostly because the victim is not always aware of what is going on. Emotional manipulators will push boundaries. They won't take no for an answer, they won't listen, and they will bulldoze their requests onto everyone else with little regard for their feelings. They fail to understand the concept of boundaries, which is why they have no problems pushing others beyond their breaking point in the relentless pursuit to get what they desire. They crowd your space physically, psychologically, and emotionally, and they care very little about how you feel about it. When someone tells them no, the manipulator doesn't listen. When you tell them that their behavior is not okay, they'll completely ignore you. Why? Because they don't care, and that is the simple truth. They don't care about anything else except their agenda. In fact, they enjoy pushing others to the limits, and they will go to any lengths to do it, including pushing past your boundaries or violating rules to do so.

They don't mind going against your wishes if doing so means they can get what they want. They may resort to behavior that includes intruding on your personal space, taking or borrowing your things without returning them, taking someone else's work and passing it off as their own, breaking promises, appointments, and even negating on agreements that were made. In some extreme cases where you might be romantically involved with a narcissistic manipulator, they could even resort to tactics that include sexual abuse or harassment, domestic violence or abuse, and even verbal and emotional abuse. The worst part of it all is some

manipulators even take pride in their behavior under the misguided notion of feeling "powerful" when they see someone else suffer at their hands.
Emotional manipulators also happen to be the biggest energy drainers because manipulators are toxic. They have a way of walking into the room and bringing with them a dark cloud of negativity, which is their way of making sure that everyone's attention becomes focused on them. People who are toxic will always suck the energy out of the room and the people that they encounter too. Whether they're feeling angry, annoyed or discontent, they want you and everyone else who might be in the room to notice, and these tactics often work because people will scramble to attend to the manipulator and ask them if they're alright or what they can do to help them feel better. The manipulator then feeds off the sympathy they are receiving from others, and by the end of it all, you feel completely emotionally exhausted, and the victim will have no idea why. The worst part of emotional manipulation and abuse is that as soon as you voice your concerns about feeling confused, overwhelmed, or under pressure, the manipulator starts paying attention. They will cunningly try to sow more seeds of doubt and make you feel as if you're incapable of handling anything if even something like this seems to make you overreact. They will try to make the victim's emotions worse in any situation, and the best thing you can do is don't let them fool you into thinking you're being dramatic.

## The Silent Treatment Is a Classic

The silent treatment is the worse emotionally abusive tactic a manipulator could pull on you. If you have been on the receiving end of the cold shoulder before, you will know how this treatment can eat away at you. Most people tend to believe that when someone is giving you the silent treatment after a disagreement, it means that they might need some time to cool off. The silent treatment is nothing more than emotional abuse, even after a disagreement. They are not "taking time to cool off," they are purposely trying to let you know that they're still "upset" with you. This prolonged period of no response is not healthy for any kind of relationship. No matter how hard you try to engage with them, they simply flat out ignore you, even when you're standing right in front of them. By completely ignoring you and pretending like you don't exist, they're trying to inflict as much emotional pain on you as they can without saying a word. They know it hurts you to be ignored, but they do it anyway. When you hit a nerve with someone or go against what they were hoping you would do, they might resort to the silent treatment if they are manipulative.
Why do manipulators, narcissists, psychopaths, sociopaths, or any of those toxic personalities love inflicting the silent treatment on others?

They're aiming to inflict as much pain as possible. Some tactics that you might witness under the silent treatment include refusal to acknowledge your existence, even when you walk into the room or sit directly in front of them. They could also refuse to engage in a conversation with you. When you try to talk to them, you're met with cold silence and a hostile glare. They refuse to make eye contact with you, even when you're doing your best to try and talk to them. If they do decide to respond, they'll choose to only use one or two sentences, keeping the response as minimal as possible and in clipped, hostile tones. If the manipulator is a narcissist, they might take things a step further. The narcissist takes things a step further by actually shaming and belittling you in public. At any opportunity to lower your self-esteem and make you feel bad, the narcissist will be willing to pounce. The lower your confidence, the more you will learn for validation and approval, which is what the narcissist wants you to feel. They want you to hang onto every word and continuously come back to them for their approval. It is a form of passive-aggressive behavior can make you feel crazy, and it is designed to show that they are "punishing you." The silent treatment emits incredibly toxic and negative energy when it's in play.

The silent treatment is not the best approach to take. It inflicts emotional trauma on the people you use it on. Being ostracized and treated like less than a person will put the other person on an emotional roller coaster, except this is a ride that is going to inflict psychological trauma on you that is so scarring it could destroy your confidence, self-esteem, and even your self-worth. The feeling of betrayal that someone you love could subject you to this kind of treatment lingers on the psyche, and depending on the intensity of the ostracism, the psychological effects can be hard to bounce back from, especially among young children.

The purpose of the silent treatment includes the following:
- **Making the Victim Wonder What They Have Done Wrong** - The victim begins worrying and wondering if they have done anything wrong. They can't stop thinking about it. If the victim happens to be an anxious person with a tendency to overthink everything, this approach is going to drive them crazy. They'll even start obsessing about what they might have done wrong (even if they haven't done anything). Pointedly ignoring someone is one way of inflicting pain without leaving any visible bruises. When we ignore or purposely exclude someone, research has indicated that it triggers a similar area in the brain, which is activated by physical pain.
- **To Avoid Looking Like the Bad Guy** - Since manipulators don't like any kind of accountability or responsibility, they would prefer to avoid looking like the bad guy. In a disagreeable situation, the one who keeps silent is often the one who ends up looking like the victim. One reason why manipulators love the

silent treatment is that it allows them to get away with their aggressive behavior while still looking like the victim, gaining the sympathy and attention from others that they wanted all along.

- **To Make the Victim Feel Guilty, and Scared** - The victim could be completely innocent, but when faced with the silent treatment, they can't help being overwhelmed by feelings of guilt. Sometimes, they might even feel scared. When the manipulator does this, they want to show the victim that they are in control. It is their indirect way of letting the victim know they have control over their emotions. Do what they want, and everything is right as rain. But if you don't do what they want, that's when the trouble starts.

- **To Get the Victim's Attention** - If the manipulator happens to be a narcissist, you can be sure the silent treatment is going to be one of their go-to techniques. They want attention from people around them because they genuinely believe the world revolves around them. In their mind, it is all about getting their needs met.

- **To Make You Worry About "Losing Them"** - They know they have influenced you enough to have you hooked. They know they've played their part well enough that you have become emotionally attached to them, and thus, the silent treatment is a way of "punishing" you and making you worry about "losing" them. The truth is, you're never going to lose them. They're not going to let you go when they know they can use you for their own benefit. This is another way of instilling fear in you by indirectly threatening that if you don't do what they want, they will walk out of your life. When you are a victim of emotional manipulation, you're blind to their faults, especially in the initial stages. They make you forget that they were the ones who pursued *you* and wanted to be in your life, not the other way around. Your life was perfectly fine before them, and given their toxic nature, your life will be better off without them too. But they have you fooled into thinking otherwise.

- **They Want You to Prioritize Their Feelings** - They want you to run around in circles worrying about how they feel. They want you to focus on keeping *them* happy, and they do this by inflicting the silent treatment on you whenever you do something that they don't agree with. They make you forget that no one has the right to barge into your life and demand that you worry about how they feel. Their feelings should not be the focal point of your day every day. Yet, victims of the silent treatment still find themselves doing this. The victims will be running around in circles, trying to keep the emotional manipulator happy while their own emotions are going topsy-turvy inside.

- **They Want to Use Apologies as A Weapon Against You -** The manipulator's apology may sound "sincere," but it is not. They *sound* like they are saying sorry, but what they are *really saying is* they are sorry they couldn't get you to do what they want. You will know when this technique is being used on you because they will apologize, but they will be giving you the cold shoulder for the next several days. They will "apologize," yet you still worry that something might be wrong or the situation wasn't fixed entirely. Another indicator that it was a fake apology is when they continue displaying the same behaviors that they were supposedly sorry for. When you confront them about it or point it out, they're going to deny it, of course. But if the silent treatment is still ongoing despite the apology, that is a sure sign it was fake.

Manipulative silent treatment tactics include the following:
- **When You Refuse to Talk Until the Other Person Gives In -** They will refuse to talk to you for as long as they feel like it. Usually, until you agree to give in to what they want. They will make you feel like it is your fault for not living up to their expectations. They can be very hypocritical, claiming that they would never do anything to hurt the victim while at the same time inflicting the silent treatment on their victim. Manipulators are hypocrites, which is why no relationship with them will ever be considered a healthy one. Manipulative partners will have no qualms about enforcing a set of rules which they expect you to follow to "make them happy," but they have no problems not abiding by the same rules they have set. They expect you to conform and do it, but they're not going to show you the same kind of courtesy because the rules don't apply to them. As soon as you don't live up to their expectations, they will pull the rug out from under you and leave you wondering what on earth went wrong.
- **When You Are Purposely Being Difficult -** Knowing that they have to make you work for their approval, affection, or attention feeds into the ego of a manipulator. When they know someone is groveling at their feet (not in a literal sense), it gives their ego and boost, and in the case of a narcissist, it makes them feel special. Manipulation is all about control, and nothing says control more than when someone else has to beg you for your time and attention.
- **Whey They Ostracize You -** As humans, we are naturally wired for a sense of belonging and community. It has been that way ever since the days of our early ancestors. We live in groups, we need to feel like we are part of a unit, and anything that ostracizes us or sets us apart is enough to affect our emotions. We are wired to feel the need to belong and connect with other

people, and this is why rejection never feels good. Rejection is pain, and this includes any form of rejection, no matter who it is from. Even if a complete stranger were to ignore you, you would still feel the pain since your brain leads you to believe you are being ostracized.

- **When They Throw Emotions Into Turmoil** - Since human emotions are volatile, it can throw the victim's emotions into a state of chaos when they are being subjected to the silent treatment. It increases the likelihood of mood swings and unpredictable behavior in some cases. The manipulator knows that when the victim is in such a state, they are incapable of thinking properly. All the manipulator has to do is wait until the victim can't take it anymore before they swoop in and deliver their ultimatum.
- **One Minute They Love You, the Next They Hate You** - Nothing messes with a person's mind more than this approach. The manipulator loves to put their victims through the wringer, tethering between love and hate. The relationship becomes a very frustrating one when the victim always must wonder whether you're going to love them or hate them today. They'll be obsessively worried and tread with trepidation around you because they don't know which way your mood is going to blow this time. This tactic can make you feel helpless because you don't know what you did wrong or how to fix it. Manipulators will tip the scales in their favor by creating a power imbalance in every discussion. This subtle trick is used to give them control while making you feel like you can't do anything about it. They waste no opportunity to remind you how important they are and the kind of influence they can have. Feeling helpless and emotionally miserable is how they control you into doing their bidding.
- **They Do It By Using Ultimatums** - To get you to go along with what they want, they force you into a corner by giving you an ultimatum that often leaves you no choice but to side with them. If the manipulator in your relationship doesn't like your friends, they could make you choose between being with them or giving up your friendship. They make you feel pressured into choosing them by instilling the fear that you might lose them if you don't. This type of manipulation can even occur in friendships, where your manipulative friend who might be jealous of a new friendship that you formed makes you choose one or the other. Someone who genuinely loved you or cared about you would never make you resort to such a thing. They would never put pressure on you to give up something they know that you loved, or that meant a lot to you.

- **They Start Blaming You For *Their* Problems** - They are inflicting the silent treatment on you because they blame you for their problems. That is what an emotional manipulator does. They are incapable of owning up to their own faults. You are always going to be the "reason" for their problems or why something went wrong, so they feel justified in giving you the silent treatment to make you feel terrible about yourself. Narcissists, in particular, can't bear to think of themselves as flawed or imperfect in any way. They will be the ones who always find someone else or something else to blame. This is an easy way out for them. It takes a lot more courage to own up to your mistakes, something the manipulator will never do because it would mean having to admit that they were flawed.

The one thing we need to clear about is that the silent treatment is inflicted *on purpose*. When someone uses this tactic on you, they know what they are doing. They know the kind of emotional and psychological damage being ignored can do you. This is not a tactic they use for fun, oh no, it isn't. This is a calculated move that is well thought out. The more the victim seeks their attention and approval, the more it feeds into their ego. By purposely using silence as their weapon of choice, they expect you to work out for yourself what's wrong and what needs to be done to fix the situation. Only when you have resolved it in a manner which they deem fit, then they will resume acknowledging and talking to you once again. Emotional scars are the ones that last a lifetime. Apologies can be made, but that doesn't mean the pain goes away completely. Emotional pain is capable of hitting you on a much deeper level than physical pain ever could. No matter what your intentions for persuasion or manipulation are, what you need to keep in mind is the damage that it could potentially cause, and whether it was worth it or not. When someone ignores you on purpose, they're trying to send a message that you're not good enough. Even if you haven't done anything wrong, the natural inclination is to feel guilty or wonder what you might have done to deserve it. No matter who does it, being on the receiving end of silent treatment can be mentally and emotionally damaging.

The Emotional Manipulator's Crazy Behaviors

Out of all the personality types, the covert narcissist has the highest tendency toward emotional manipulation. Now, these behavioral traits are not exclusive to the narcissist alone. Other types of emotionally abusive personalities may display some of these common characteristics too. If any of these traits resonate with you, you could have been covertly manipulating other people's emotions without even realizing it.

- **The "Word Salad" Game** - Conversations that don't make any sense are a favorite mind game of the malignant narcissist. Word salad is when a person uses a jumble of words and throws them together for no rhyme or reason with no structure, purpose, or coherence. Word salad conversations are often nonsensical, and what you're left with is utter nonsense and an argument that is unreasonable. They're just trying to confuse and frustrate you enough to the point where you eventually give up and give in to what they want when you can no longer take the frustration anymore. Attempts at disorienting and confusing you are a favorite tactic whenever the narcissist believes that they are about to lose an argument, or when they believe you are challenging or disagreeing with them. They aim to discredit and frustrate you, and the longer you stand there trying to have a rational conversation with them, the more frustrated and drained you will begin to feel. When you're at your lowest point, but you still try to stand your ground anyway, they whip out the silent treatment, ignoring you until you finally can't take it anymore and give in to them.

- **They Make You Feel Crazy** - When you're already going crazy trying to figure out what went wrong and why you're being subjected to the silent treatment, they come in and make you feel even crazier by gaslighting any points or arguments you may point out. With the silent treatment, you're already questioning yourself and feeling guilty, even when you have no idea what is wrong. Gaslighting your points will only make the situation worse. But of course, that is what the manipulator wanted all along. The "crazier" and less confident you feel, the better it is for them. When someone makes you question your sanity, it can have a tremendous impact on your confidence, self-esteem, and ability to trust anyone else. This paranoia can last for years, and the rest of your relationships are going to be the ones that suffer the consequences.
- **Nitpicking to A Fault** - Imagine if someone was always pointing out your flaws and everything that is wrong in your life. First, they point out your flaws, and then ignore you to make it sting even more. They will nitpick every single detail so much that it becomes destructive and bordering on a personal attack. Narcissists will lead you to believe you're not good enough for the impossible standards, and their comments are not meant to help you, but rather criticize you and make you feel unworthy. They make you feel even worse when they choose to ignore you after pointing out your flaws. But, a few hours or a few days later, they start talking to you as per normal, like nothing happened. This emotional yo-yo that they put you on can negatively impact your psyche in the long run.

# Other Emotional Manipulation Techniques

Emotional manipulation is enough to drive anyone crazy. The worries that go on and on in your mind, day in and day out, are enough to make anyone feel like they are losing their marbles. That is what being subjected to the silent treatment will do. It makes you question yourself and worry about whether you're the problem. This is what these calculative, conniving emotional abusers want from you. The less confident you are, the easier you become as a target of their deception. It makes you desperate for forgiveness that you would be willing to say and do anything, even things you normally wouldn't do, just to get your partner to accept you again. It makes you second-guess yourself, and it causes you to doubt your self-worth, and being desperate for acceptance and love might make you become somebody that you're not. It makes you become somebody that they approve of or expect, even when you don't recognize who this new version of yourself is.

Here are the most common emotionally manipulative tactics:

- **Find A Way To Be The "Victim"** - This is the way most manipulators operate. They find a way to always be the "victim." The whole world feels sorry for them. Manipulators can easily trick the people around them into believing that they need them. In truth, the manipulator's pretend helplessness is nothing more than a ruse to mislead you into doing what they want. Pretending to be the victim is their subtle way of indirectly telling you that you *cannot* leave them, or they will crumble and fall without you. Not true at all. The only reason they want you around is that you're useful to them. They will always appear to be the "victim" because they can twist and turn their words so well. To make themselves appear blameless and innocent, the manipulator will always twist and turn your words to distort what really happened. It will always be to their benefit, never yours. Somehow, they end up making you feel like the one who is in the wrong, and you are the one who walks away feeling guilty even though you had every right to voice your discontent.
- **Appear Superior** - Snide remarks, criticism, and pedant are a few ways to emotionally manipulate your victim into believing they are not good enough. If they are exposed to this kind of behavior over a sustained period, it won't be long before it eventually begins to chip away at their self-confidence. The less confident they are, the easier they become to control. Emotional manipulators are often arrogant and narcissistic, acting in a superior manner towards everyone around them. To make you feel inferior, they will overwhelm you with data all at once, especially in the workplace, and often about subjects or pieces of the data that you don't know of, making you feel insecure about falling behind.

- **Triangulation** - Another tactic to play on the victim's emotions is to say nasty things that make them feel bad about themselves. Driving wedges between people is one way of separating the victim from the rest of their social circle. When the victim feels "isolated" from everyone else, they become a lot easier to manipulate.
- **A Blast of Emotion** - The quickest way to make the people around you feel uncomfortable enough to agree with you (depending on the situation and circumstance) is to have an emotional blow up. An outburst of emotion makes people feel uncomfortable because they don't always know how to react. When you produce a highly emotional reaction, like a burst of anger or an outpouring of tears, people will be less reluctant to ask questions and try to poke holes in your requests.
- **Project** - This emotionally manipulative tactic happens when you project an air of perfection and make it seem like other people have all the flaws. By creating a false sense of discord, you will try to make you and everyone else feel like they owe you a favor. With this manipulative tactic, you don't want to take ownership of your mistakes because you don't believe you're at fault. That is what an emotional manipulator tends to do. Project an air of perfection and let other people believe they are the ones in the wrong all the time.

**Purposely Misunderstanding** - If you want to make your victims feel frustrated, you need to pretend that you purposely misunderstand them. Emotional manipulators who use this tactic tend to spread falsehoods and wrong ideas about their victims. They do this on purpose to make the victim look bad. Manipulators will attempt to create confusion and misunderstanding by making sweeping generalizations and blanket statements that often have no factual basis. Exaggerations aimed at invalidating the victim's experience are how they try to maintain the upper hand against their opponents. Repeatedly telling your victim that you've misunderstood is a deceptive way of undermining their communication skills, making them doubt their own ability to. Let it go on for long enough, and they will lose their confidence to speak up for fear of being misunderstood again. This creates even more frustration in your victims by deliberately misrepresenting their feelings and thoughts until it becomes almost absurd. Instead of respecting their opinions and emotions, turn them into character flaws if it doesn't align with your own agenda. That is how you become emotionally manipulative. Weaving and spinning tales to reframe what it is you're really trying to say is what manipulators do best.

- **Flirting** - Oh yes, flirting can be considered an emotionally manipulative tactic. Some people can be naturally charming, but it is the ones who are too charming that you want to watch out for. Flirting with someone could be as simple as constantly flattering them with praise even for the simplest of items. Flirt and use charm to get what you want, and some people will go to any lengths to stroke your ego just to get you on their side. When you flirt with someone to get what you want, you're manipulating them. Be careful not to overdo this tactic, though, since once it starts to feel too much, the victims will be on their guard and think you might be up to something sneaky.
- **Intimidation** - This manipulative tactic calls for the spread of fear among the people you are trying to control. Do you notice how in a toxic work environment, there are some managers or bosses who instill fear in the hearts of their victims? When that boss or manager rolls around, it is pin-drop silence. That is what happens when you employ the use of fear as a manipulative tactic. When people are afraid of you, they will also be too afraid to disagree with you. Manipulators will try and use this tactic to instill either extreme fear or discomfort in their victim and put enough pressure on their victims until they will quickly succumb to their bidding just to escape the emotional abuse. For example, they could raise their voice when you try to push back against their suggestion. They could display temper tantrums when you try to reject their requests. They condescend, they belittle, and they talk down to you and make you feel small and insignificant. They make it clear that they are superior while everyone else is simply inferior. As soon as the victim feels small and starts to question their confidence, that is when you swoop in for the kill.
- **False Promises** - Nothing creates more stress and frustration in the victim than when the manipulator never follows through with what they promised, and then they conveniently fail to follow through at the last minute, you could be a victim of manipulation. They are skilled at "forgetting" what the promises that they made, denying that they ever said anything at all, and you must be the one who is mistaken. With no recording or documented proof to hold them to it, they pin the excuse on your poor memory, perhaps even resorting to calling you an outright liar. So skilled are they at this tactic that they make you start to doubt yourself and wonder if perhaps you could have been mistaken after all.
- **Taunting** - Keep taunting your victim by moving their "goalposts." This is another attempt at making them feel inadequate. When someone proudly tells you how they accomplish one goal that they set out to do, you'll come back with something else that you haven't accomplished. If your victim

points out how they finally got promoted or achieved the success they wanted for your career, you will come right back by pointing out how they are not a millionaire yet.

# CHAPTER 4
## *Make Them Agree If You Want Them To*

Think about a person that you know in your life that you disagree with. Think about this person disagreeing with you on a subject that matters to you. The kind of disagreement that could potentially spark an argument. Perhaps an argument that is explosive enough to end a friendship. Why do we find it so hard to get other people to say yes to what we want? There could be several reasons for that. One of those reasons is that you're not actively listening to them. While you may be "listening" to what they say, what you're really listening for is the opportunity to refute whatever they say. They are doing the same thing. Instead of listening actively to better understand each other, we're listening for opportunities to rebuke each other's claims. No wonder we find it so hard to convince people to say yes when we want them to. We've been going about it the wrong way.

Everyone is guilty of this. It's not that we are doing it on purpose, but it is because everyone has a natural tendency to prioritize their needs before everyone else's. We want other people to listen to *us*. We want them to nod along to whatever we say. But are we extending the same treatment towards them? Everything you are expecting out of a conversation, they are expecting the same thing. Most people reading this book assume they are open-minded and flexible. But, truth be told, you might not be as open-minded as you think you are. If you sometimes feel the need to resort to manipulative tactics because you feel you're not being listened to enough, then you're probably not as open-minded or flexible as you would like to believe. You and many other people out there find it hard to say yes to each other because we're not willing to change what we believe in so easily. Even when we are faced with the facts, it can be hard to change.

Change is never an easy thing. Changing our minds about something we believe is important to us will take time. It takes a lot of effort and a lot of trust to change your mind. This is something you need to keep in mind when you're attempting to get other people to say yes to you when you want them to. Just because you want them to change their minds *right now*, doesn't mean it is going to happen. Trust takes time, don't get frustrated with them if they need a little more convincing. Getting someone to say yes to you requires not only trust but also empathy, patience, vulnerability, and, most of all, it needs *courage*. The ability to change someone's mind is a skill.

## There Is A Science to Saying Yes

Persuasion is a subject that has been studied by researchers for a long time. It would be nice to think that we consider all the available data before we make a decision. The truth is, our brains have a lot more to do with persuasion than we think. Your brain may have enormous power, but it also contains weaknesses, and that weakness is the fact that it can easily be influenced and manipulated. That you can be persuaded to say yes, if you know how to push without being pushy. If you think about it, that's what manipulators are doing already to get their way. They're relying on a few subconscious techniques to get almost anything they want, and they're using these subconscious techniques on you because they know how the brain works, and which emotional buttons to push to make you feel a certain way. The human brain today suffers from information overload, and therefore, it now seeks shortcuts or rules of thumb that it can quickly fall back on to make a decision.

In his book entitled *Influence: The Psychology of Persuasion* by Robert B. Cialdini, Cialdini talks about a study that was conducted on North American turkeys. Mother turkeys are extremely instinctive when it comes to protecting their young. But the reaction and care of the mother turkey are contingent on one thing: *The "cheap-cheap" sound that their chicks make*. The appearance and scent of the chicks don't make much difference to the other. On if the chicks emitted the cheap-cheap sound would the mother turkey care of it. Chicks that didn't make the sound would be ignored or neglected. The mother turkey is fiercely protective of those it recognizes as its offspring. Any sign of intrusion and the mother would react viciously to protect their chicks. An experiment was done to test the limits of the turkey's perception. In the experiment, a stuffed toy predator was pulled along on a string within the mother turkey's proximity. Immediately, the mother turkey reacted aggressively and proceeded to attack the "intruder." However, when the stuffed toy was embedded with a recording of the chick's cheap-cheap sound, the mother turkey welcomed the predator with open arms. This action is classified as a *Fixed-Action Pattern*. It is a pattern of behavior that is prevalent in all creatures.

A principle fixed-action pattern in human behavior that is well-known is the *"favor for a favor"* exchange. Basically, if you want people to say yes, you need to *give them a reason* to say yes in the first place. They need to know what is in it for them and how they are going to benefit by saying yes to you. Persuasion is essentially a psychological trick of the mind. Millions of people around the world are constantly persuading and manipulating others and experiencing great success with it too. Again, it boils down to understanding the workings of the human mind and what makes them tick. Manipulators rely on communication as their main persuasive strategy. We communicate so often that we do it almost without thinking. It is as natural to us as breathing, and many times we have found ourselves saying things we don't mean because we're not actively thinking about our communication process. It is not just the words that are being said, but the way that we say them too.

The human brain wants to avoid guilt and has a fixed-action pattern because it works in two different parts when it comes to the decision-making process. The two parts of the brain are the conscious and the subconscious mind. Your conscious mind is the adult, while your subconscious mind is like that of a child. Think of the conscious mind as the gatekeeper for the unconscious mind. It is designed to filter data before that data has a chance to reach your subconscious mind. We're constantly feeding our subconscious with data. So much of the subconscious thought process happens on autopilot. Napoleon Hill first pioneered the idea of positive thinking when he observed that the subconscious mind does not distinguish between destructive and constructive thoughts. Hill believed that the mind is capable of translating a thought driven by fear into reality as much as it can translate a thought driven by faith or courage into a positive outcome. It is up to us to make the distinction. Manipulators slip past your conscious mind with clever use of several word combinations to charm and beguile you, blinding you to their real intentions. They might even give the impression that they're brilliant, they're so charming and articulate when they speak. When the manipulator uses these words in a Machiavellian way, these words can pierce through almost everything.

## Universal Rules That Coax Someone Into Saying Yes

Now, earlier, it was touched on how the human brain actively seeks shortcuts to help it arrive at a decision much faster, given the information overload we are exposed to daily. Universally, these are the shortcuts that everyone falls back on to help them decide whether they should say yes or no:
- Reciprocity
- Scarcity
- Authority
- Consistency
- Liking
- Consensus

Once you know how these shortcuts work on manipulating the mind into saying yes, you significantly increase your chances of getting them to say yes when you want them to.
- **Reciprocity** is the obligation that we feel to give back to others when someone has done us a favor, given us a gift, or provided a service that we are grateful for. When you're invited to a party by a friend, you feel obligated to invite them to the next party you are hosting at your house. People are a lot more likely to say yes to you when they feel like they are indebted to you. Therefore, if you want them to say yes, you need to give them a "gift" of some sort

that will make it difficult for them to reject you when it comes time to return the favor.
- ***Scarcity*** is a principle that works on the basis of "when you have less, you want more." This is why "sale" or "limited edition" marketing tactics tend to work so well, especially the latter. When someone is limited, your brain automatically tells you that you *must* have it because you don't want to avoid missing out. There is a term for this condition too, and it is called the *Fear of Missing Out (FOMO)*. In 2003, when British Airways announced that the twice-daily Concorde flight from London to New York would not be operating anymore because it had become "uneconomical," sales skyrocketed the very next day. Nothing had changed about the Concorde flight. It wasn't flying better or faster. The service remained the same. Sales skyrocketed because customers were now seeing it as a "scarce resource." Instill the FOMO in your persuasive techniques, and you will have people clambering to say yes to you.
- ***Authority*** means people will be more willing to say yes to you when they believe you are an authority on the subject. This one is easy enough to implement because all you need to do is position yourself as an expert on the subject, and they will be inclined to believe what you tell them. Do you notice how people automatically obliged to the requests of anyone who wears an authoritative uniform? They do it without even asking. This signals that it is important to let others know why you are a credible authority even before you put forth your request. Since you're probably not going to wear a uniform when you persuade them, your best approach would be to appear confident when you're presenting your facts.
- ***Consistency*** - People are likely to respond warmly when they can relate to the consistencies in your request. Our brains love familiarity, and the idea here to get them to familiarize themselves with saying yes to you. To do this, you need to present them with smaller requests and commitments, they have an easier time agreeing too. For example, when you start with smaller favors like asking to borrow a pen or asking your colleague to do you a favor and grab a cup of coffee for you too since they are already going out to get one anyway. This opens their mind to the idea that agreeing with you is not that difficult after all when they could easily comply with the requests you presented them with. A masterful persuasive individual would start with the smaller favors before working their way up.
- ***Liking*** focuses on how people are a lot more likely to say yes to you if they already like you. If they don't like you, their reluctance is going to make it very difficult for them to oblige to your

requests, even if they know it is going to be for their benefit. Would you find it easy to say yes to someone you didn't like? Probably not. The brain likes people who are similar to us, people who cooperate with us, and people who give us compliments. Before you begin your persuasion, start by seeking similarities that you can use as a way to connect with them. If you start that way, there is a 90% chance that you are going to be a lot more successful in your interactions with them. The principle of "liking" is a powerful tactic that you should be tapping into. Focus on areas of similarity that you share and direct their attention toward that as a start. Once they're warmed up and excited about having a subject they can use to connect with you, that is when you slowly ease your request into the picture. Don't forget about throwing in some genuine compliments before you get down to business.

- **Consensus** matters the most when they are uncertain or hesitant about saying yes. In general, people look at the behaviors and actions of others to help them decide what to do. For example, if you told someone that 75% of the people you have persuaded to hop on board with your idea were thrilled with the success they have had, you're pointing out what a good idea your suggestion is. This makes it a lot harder for them to resist since their brains are going to latch onto the fact that 75% of people you're influenced are already successful. They will want to be part of that number, and this increases your odds of getting a resounding yes out of them.

## Why People Say No to You

There is nothing more frustrating than having someone say no when you *need them to say yes*. Sometimes, we might be so desperate for them to say yes that we end up making several costly mistakes along the way. We have all had someone say no to us at one point or another. It never feels good, and sometimes it feels downright terrible. You end up feeling frustrated, wondering what you could have done differently to change the situation. If you're wondering why people say no to you, it could be because of the following mistakes:

- **What You Tell Them Doesn't Grab Attention** - If the things you are telling them are boring, they're not going to be interested, let alone want to say yes. When you don't make a powerful impression right away, you're unlikely to have the power to persuade them the way that you need to. First impressions are made within the first 30-seconds of meeting someone. That is when you pretty much start to form your first impressions about them. If your first impression doesn't start off strong and immediately grabs their attention, they're not going to be interested in what you have to say. People naturally pay attention to those who give off an air of confidence. When you're confident, you automatically give the impression that everything you have to say is important. If you want them to say yes, it is time to start paying attention to your confidence, the way you approach others, and your body language. These are key factors if you want them to pay more attention to you when you're talking.

- **You're Too Desperate** - As much as you may be desperate for them to say yes, avoid making it obvious. People will do the opposite of what you want them to if they can sense your desperation. Your desperation could be the reason why you're coming off as too pushy or bossy at times. Plus, it is not doing your confidence any favors either. The approach that you should take instead is to appear calm and nonchalant like it doesn't matter whether they say yes or no. Adopting this approach will remind you to take a step back and give them some space to avoid coming off too strong. Present your points, but take a step back and allow them to come to you.

- **You Seem Negative** - Nothing turns people away faster than someone who gives off an air of negativity. If you think you're doing a good job of concealing it and pretending to be happy, you're probably not. That is because negativity is a very powerful, all-consuming emotion. If you are negative, it is going to show through, and this will quickly turn people away from you. You cannot present your points in a neutral, logical manner when your mindset has been clouded by negative perceptions even before you started. Your views and contributions will have elements of negativity in them, and it is going to be obvious to the listening party. Remember, they are *looking* for reasons to reject your claims. A negative pessimist is not a fun person to be around, and the last person that anyone will be seeking advice from.

- **You Sound Like You're Bragging** - Since you want them to say yes so badly, you could be at risk of making this mistake: *You sound like you are bragging too much.* Conversations tend to go south when you start humblebragging. That's a mistake to stay away from. Some people make the mistake of trying to impress others with their humblebrag, not realizing that it actually has the opposite effect. Imagine if you had to strike up a conversation with someone who proceeds to talk about how busy, chaotic, or fabulous their life is? They go on and on about how their job forces them to travel all over the world, or how they've been asked to take on the leadership position even though they would rather stay out of the spotlight. People will probably be listening politely and nodding along, but at the same time, they are looking for a way to end the conversation. Even with the best intentions, these conversations never pan out well because it makes it seem as though you're trying to appear superior, and the other person feels inferior. Best to stick to the factual points and let the facts speak for themselves.

- **You Try Too Hard to Be Liked** - Trying too hard is just as bad as coming off too strong. When people sense that you're trying way too hard to be liked, they end up moving further away from you. People have an uncanny ability to spot desperation from a mile away. People pleasers are not much fun to be around because they give the impression of being too clingy or needy. People will stay away from you if they sense you have any of these two traits. Pulse, when you try too hard to be liked, it makes it seem like you're willing to say anything to get them to like you. That will not instill a lot of confidence in them, and thus, they're not going to say yes to you. Stay calm and be yourself, don't try too hard even if you desperately want them to say yes to you. They eventually will if you use the right techniques on them (we'll talk about that in a bit). Tone down your intensity and save your intense passion for another time.
- **You're Too Intense** - Your passion for the subject is a good thing, but too much of a good thing can backfire when you're trying to persuade others to go along with what you want. Passion is great, and it is commendable that you have such a strong belief system you're willing to stand by. But too much intensity is not the best approach to take when you're trying to convince someone to change their mind and swing over to your side. Being too intense could make you prone to arguments when someone tries to refute your points. Arguments will only drive people away.
- **You're Not Expressive Enough When You Speak** - Being too intense is not a good thing, but not being expressive enough is just as bad. Imagine having a conversation with someone who stares blankly at you the whole time. When we're trying to persuade someone, we often rely on their facial expressions and eye contact to determine how well the conversation is going. Having someone stare blankly back at you while you're trying your best to engage with them is not a good sign. While you are trying to gauge their feelings by reading their facial expressions, you can be sure that they are doing the same thing to you. If you don't convey the right expressions that support your points, you're not going to be convincing enough to win them over. When they smile, we know it's going well. If they mirror our expressions and mannerisms, it's definitely going well. But if their brow is furrowed, creased, or they simply look bored and disinterested, it's safe to say they are not interested in prolonging the

conversation right now. When you're trying to leave a good impression, don't forget to use your facial expressions to signal to them how well the conversation is going.
- **You Have A Reputation for Being Non-Committal** - This is a case of your past coming back to haunt you, although this isn't going to happen all the time. But if you're trying to convince people who happen to run in the same circles and they know a little about your history, they're going to be hesitant to say yes if you have a reputation for being non-committal. Never following through on your promises is a bad thing. Not being on time is a bad thing. Canceling with no warning is a bad thing. People will talk, and word will spread. That is why it is so important to stick to your word when you've given it because, in some cases, your past can come back to bite you when you least expect it. All it takes is for news to spread unfavorably, and your chances of being persuasive or convincing are going to double or triple in difficulty. People will be driven away by your "boy who cried wolf" reputation. If you give your word, you better be able to stick to it.
- **You Don't Respect Their Personal Space** - Unless you're with immediate family or very close friends, you should respect a person's personal space when you're communicating with them. Too close and you make the other person feel uncomfortable, too far, and you come off as disinterested. You need to pay close attention to the person you are talking to and watch for signs of discomfort. Even if you're trying to be friendly, invading personal spaces can come off as annoying, aggressive, or just plain rude. Standing too close to someone makes them feel uncomfortable because you're invading their personal space. The concept of personal space is an important part of non-verbal communication. As soon as you notice that they are not comfortable with your proximity, take a few steps back to create a comfortable enough space between the two of you. You want to make sure you're leaving at least two feet of space and not invading their personal bubble. Watch out for your personal space, because it could very well be the tipping point that lands you a new friend, relationship, or a new job.
- **You're Too Opinionated** - Being a know-it-all is not a cool thing to be proud of, even if you have all the answers to everything. Shouting it from the rooftops by being too opinionated is not going to persuade anyone to follow you. In fact, it is going to convince them to avoid you. Being too opinionated is an annoying trait because it makes other people feel dumb or inferior to you. This is not the best way to convince them to join your team. When people come to you with a question or something they want to talk about, most of the time, they just

want someone to talk to. They're not specifically looking for a solution unless they say so. If you're too busy dishing out your opinions, thinking you have the answers to all their problems, they're not going to be thrilled about going along with what you want. People don't like to be told what to do, even if they don't admit this out loud to themselves. They just want someone to listen to them while they vent their feelings, emotions, and frustrations.

- **You're Behaving Selfishly** - This is why manipulators will never have success for long. Eventually, once people realize their true colors and how selfishly they are behaving, they'll quickly turn away from the manipulator and avoid them at all costs. Nobody wants to be around someone who only cares about themselves. You will be the last person they want to agree with if you adopt this approach. When you constantly prioritize your points of view without considering how they think or feel, it shows you are only interested in fulfilling your own agenda. People don't like this, and they will never follow you once they know this is who you are. Learn to consider the opinions of others, and it will win you a lot more brownie points in the long run.
- **You Are Not Honest** - Telling lies in a bid to guard your privacy is only going to work if you're absolutely sure no one is going to find out what you're up to. No one is going to say yes to someone who is shady, and someone that they feel they cannot put their trust in. Being open, honest, and transparent in everything you say will show the other person that can be trusted. That you act with integrity and honesty, and this will help to strengthen their trust in you because you mean what you say, and you say what you mean. Trust and respect go a long way in successful and effective persuasion, and if other people can't respect you or trust you, you will be doomed right from the start with no hope of success. The minute they think you are a liar, they begin to question if they can trust you. Would you take advice from someone you don't trust? Probably not.
- **You're Not Assertive Enough** - People might overlook you if you are not assertive enough when you're trying to convince them. Assertiveness is not about being loud and getting in their faces, demanding that they listen to you. Assertiveness is being able to stand firm on your opinion while still being able to convey your thoughts and points of view in an appropriate manner if you are in a work situation. Assertiveness is about speaking in a way that they can relate to. It is the *only effective way* to make yourself heard without committing any of the other mistakes above. Being assertive and calm during a conversation will give you the assurance that you are in control of the situation,

especially when you've got your limits to guide you and let you know what lines you're not willing to cross.

## Foolproof Ways to Change Someone's Mind

Maybe you've tried it in the past, and it hasn't worked. But that might be because you haven't tried these foolproof techniques to change someone's mind and get them to say *yes* when you want them to. Perhaps in the past, you were hesitant about trying to influence someone enough to change their mind without having to resort to drastic manipulation. This is understandable enough since there is a genuine cause for concern. When you try too hard to get someone to go along with you, you run the risk of ruining the relationship if it doesn't go according to plan. Hence the need for these techniques. How do you get someone to say *yes* when you want them to? By employing the following approach:

- **Don't Turn Conversations into Arguments** - Getting frustrated when someone refuses you is something we have all been guilty of. What you should do instead of present the data you have in a way that doesn't hurt or hinder their opinions. Don't make it seem obvious that you are trying to get them to change their minds. If you can stay calm and present your point logically, they will eventually see things from your point of view. After all, it can be hard to argue against logic and cold-hard facts. Staying calm is the tricky part since our emotions can sometimes get the best of us. Emotions are going to impact both parties. If the other person you are trying to convince has a lot of pride and ego, those emotions are going to make them resistant to agreeing with you simply because they want to be right. Escalating the conversation into an argument certainly won't help your cause. Always keep the conversation as calm and neutral as possible, even when the other person is starting to get emotional. Fight your urge to combat emotion with emotion. There is no winning if you take that approach.
- **Get Them to Say *Yes* as Quickly As Possible** - Start by emphasizing and keep emphasizing points that can be agreed upon as soon as you start the conversation. Throughout the conversation, keep emphasizing the points that *you* want them to agree on with you. Start the conversation strong by talking about things that you know they would agree on, like their favorite hobbies or whether they watched Game of Thrones yet. If you can start by getting them to agree with you on several points right from the start, they are a lot more likely to say *yes* when you deliver the finishing touch. This foot-in-the-door technique is actually a common sales technique used by the savviest and top-performing salespeople. You're not manipulating them too

drastically, but you are subtly influencing their minds from the start to make it seem like you're an agreeable person. When you start the conversation with topics of interest that they can agree with, it makes them like you. When they like you, they open up to you. When they open up to you, they become a lot more accepting of your ideas.

- **Don't Tell Them You Were Wrong** - Even if you are wrong, don't tell them that. At least, not unless there is a genuine need for it. Telling someone you are wrong immediately makes you seem less credible in their mind. The minute they hear you say that they are going to think they were right not to go along with what you wanted. When you tell them you were wrong, you're giving them a strong reason to combat your arguments and resist you even more. Don't give them that opportunity to topple your arguments and let the power swing over to their side. Even if you present a lot of facts and data *after* you have admitted you're wrong, it is not going to make a difference. Once their brain latches onto the notion that you're wrong and you admitted you were wrong, that is the only thing they are going to focus on. No, keep the power in your control by still presenting a calm exterior, even if you happen to be wrong on one or two points. Never let them see you sweat. No one will know that you're wrong if you act like nothing's wrong. It all comes down to carrying yourself with confidence. If you want to change their mind, you have to avoid *looking like you are trying to change their mind*. Even if you are trying to prove them wrong, don't give the game away by making it obvious. You can ensure that the power always stays on your side by being the only person who is completely aware and in control of the conversation at all times.

- **Let Them Do A Lot Of the Talking** - This is a classic mistake that trips most people up. When you're trying to convince someone, you *are not the one* who should be doing all the talking. *They are*. If you let them do all the talking, it gives the appearance that you care more about their opinion and their feelings. It leads them to believe you genuinely care about what they have to say, and thus, they will be a lot more receptive in return when it is your turn to talk. People *love* the idea that other people are interested in what they have to say. That is because most people enjoy conversations, and they want other people to know their ideas and opinions. Listening to them feeds into their head of wanting to be heard. You're going to make them feel friendlier towards you, and they will start trusting you more when you tell them something. Let them do all the talking and pay attention to them. They will reciprocate when it's your turn to talk. One crucial tip to remember here is that even if you happen to disagree with something they say, *never interrupt them* while they are talking. This is a very risky move as it could immediately lead to a change in perception about you. People don't like to be disagreed with in general, and if you interrupt them while they're talking, they're going to shut down and turn away from you. Interruptions and pointing out that you disagree with them is like a personal attack on their ego (depending on the individual in question, of course). Another thing you could do is to agree with their opinions while you're at it. Since nobody likes to feel pressured into doing anything, you'll have an easier time convincing them if you agree with their perspective every now and then. Validating their feelings lets them know that how they feel matters to you, and that you're not simply trying to cram an idea down their throat for your own benefit. The best strategy is to be patient and listen to them with an open mind. Encourage them to talk as much as possible and the best active listener you can be.

- **Make Them Believe They Came Up With the Idea Themselves -** This Jedi-like mind trick is guaranteed to get them to agree with you and say *yes* when you want them to. There is a very simple reason why this mind trick works so well. People are easier to convince when they believe that they arrived at the solution on their own. Even if it was through your gentle guidance that steered them in the right direction, let the final decision rest with them, allowing them to believe that it was their idea all along. One effective approach would be to get them to list the pros and cons and then asking them which they believe would be the best approach to take from there. If you think about it, you tend to have more faith in ideas if you were the one who came up with them as opposed to if you heard them from someone else. Instead of telling them outright *why* they should agree with you, this is by far the smarter approach to take. It is the smarter approach to make the "suggestion" and then let them believe they reached the decision on their own. People feel pride when they think they came up with an awesome idea, and this is one way of stroking their ego while you're at it. When you let them arrive at a conclusion themselves, it makes them feel like the idea was theirs, even if you were the one who suggested it.

# CHAPTER 5
## Under Your Spell

What happens when someone is hypnotized? We've all seen those individuals who claim to be hypnotists. We've even seen them on magic shows or performing on the streets where they attempt to hypnotize the crowd. Perhaps the most commonly used hypnotist trick that we are all familiar with is when they swing a watch in front of us, telling us to keep a close watch while they tell us our eyes gradually feel heavier and heavier. We're getting sleepy, and when they snap their fingers, we're suddenly under their spell, doing what they want us to do. You've probably seen this trick so many times that you don't think about it too much anymore. We have become accustomed to the idea that hypnotists can make people fall asleep on command, hop around on one foot, or quack like a duck if we wanted them to.

But is there more to hypnotism than meets the eye? Is there really power to be found in a soothing voice and a watch swinging in front of your face? Maybe there is more to hypnosis than the simple party trick we initially believed it was.

## What Is Hypnosis

Modern hypnosis started sometime in the 1700s, and it all began with a man named Franz Mesmer. Interestingly enough, this is where we get the term "mesmerized" from. Mesmer believed in a theory called *animal magnetism,* and he was not referring to sex appeal either. Mesmer believed that every living creature had invisible, magnetic fluids that flowed through them. Mesmer claimed that he could help to cure people of all sorts of ailments by simply adjusting that magnetic flow. He would use dim lights, flashy hand gestures, and ethereal-like music to put some of his clients in a trance-like state. However, when scientists put his magnetic fluid theory to the test, they found that it wasn't a real thing. Mesmer and his research were discredited, even though some of his patients did claim that they felt better after a treatment session or two with him. Sometime in the mid-1800s, James Braid, a surgeon at the time, picked up on this research and began to study it. He used the term *"hypnosis"* to describe what Mesmer was doing, a term that originated from the Greek word *"Hypnos."* In today's modern world, some psychologists believe that hypnosis only seems like drowsiness, but in reality, hypnosis is a focused psychological state of mind. Very similar to mediation.

As a surreal concept, hypnosis has been shrouded by misconceptions and myths. People are still scared of it despite scientific research showing the connection of the practice to how the mind behaves. Hypnosis is not a recent innovation of the New Age movement that came about in the 1970s and 1980s. In the United States, at least, hypnosis was already part of the medical world's lingo back in the mid-1800s. Sigmund Freud, Pierre Janet, and Alfred Binet were some of the pioneers of this mental condition. To understand hypnotism is to understand the history of it from ancient times to modern psychologists, researchers, and physicians.

## Hypnosis Through the Ages

The earliest forms of healing evidence with hypnosis is written in Egyptian Ebers Papyrus, dating to 1550 BC. Another Egyptian papyrus (Pap. A. Nr. 65) from around the 3rd century CE explains how a practitioner's hands are laid on the patient to promote hypnosis, concentration, and relaxation. Ancient cultures ranging from the Persian, Sumerian, Indian, Chinese, Greek, Egyptian, and Roman have used some form of hypnosis. The sick in Egypt and Greece often went to places of healing that are known as dream temples or sleep temples, where hypnosis was used to cure their ailments. The Sanskrit book in ancient India, known as *The Law of Manu* explains how different levels of hypnosis are used like "Sleep-Waking," "Dream-Sleep," and "Ecstasy-Sleep."

In the Middle Ages, it was believed that kings, princes, and royals had healing powers, and the term *Royal Touch* was used because it was attributed to divine powers. Before the term hypnosis was even used, it was referred to as 'magnetism' and 'mesmerism' to describe the healing by hypnosis. Paracelsus, the Swiss physician, was among the first to use magnets as a method of healing, instead of using holy relics or the divine touch. This method of healing was used until the 18th century when Maximillian Hell, a Jesuit priest and the Royal Astronomer in Vienna, started using magnetized steel plates on the body, which then became a popular form of healing. Among Hell's students was none other than Franz Mesmer, who is an Austrian physician. He began using the term "mesmerize" to explain and describe this form of healing. Mesmer soon found out that he could induce a state of trance without using magnets, and concluded (incorrectly) that he had the ability to heal instead.

The Marquis de Puysegur, who was one of Mesmer's students, soon became a successful magnetism and also the first person to produce a deeper form of hypnosis that is akin to a sleep-walking. Soon, followers of Paracelsus-Mesmer's "Fluid-ism" Theory and Puysegur started referring to themselves as *Experimentalists*. The work produced by the Experimentalists and Mesmer was a step towards the right direction of hypnotism, where it recognizes the cures that were a result not from an object or a magnet but from a different force altogether.

## Meditation versus Hypnosis

At first glance, meditation and hypnosis seem like two concepts that have nothing in common. One is all about sitting calmly and trying to find your inner peace while the other is full of flashy hand gestures and elaborate techniques to try and convince you that mind control is possible. But there are similarities that meditation and hypnosis do share, and those similarities are how both practices have a certain degree of influence on our brains. Some researchers believe that hypnosis is capable of creating changes in your brain. Some psychologists even use this technique to help their patients as part of their therapy. Hypnosis is very real, but not in the overly exaggerated manner that we are used to thinking of. Hypnosis is a mental condition that has been in our world for more than two hundred years. Despite that, scientific experts have yet to uncover how our brain, use of words and actions influence and manipulate the way we do things. Meditation is one example of a form of hypnosis since you can train your mind to enter a trance-like state when you practice it. Buddhist monks have used meditation as one approach to detach themselves from their thoughts and meditation has proven time and time again what an effective tool it can be to help us practice mindful awareness.

When scientists studied the brains of Buddhist monks, they discovered that the region of the brain associated with empathy was a lot more pronounced in the monks who had been regularly meditating for years. The higher Alpha waves in the minds of these meditators reduced the number of negative emotions experienced. Studies conducted have discovered that after 8- weeks of meditation, gray matter in the brain was denser in areas associated with learning, emotional regulation, and memory processing. The amygdala, however, which deals with blood pressure and stress, experienced a decrease in brain matter.

Meditation is probably the single most important skill you can learn in a world today where stressful stimuli come at you from all angles. Not to mention that it points out the human mind is capable of change, and it can be controlled when you have the right techniques to do it. Human beings are the species with the most highly developed brain on the planet, and because of that, we're given the gift of being able to create things. We create technology. We create inventions that make our lives a little bit easier. We've helped to shape the planet into what it is today. Our brain is so powerful that we can even reshape our reality by simply learning how to quiet the mind and change our brains. Meditation allows your mind to explore this side of your natural state, the stillness that is true and pure. There are a lot of benefits to mediation. Frequent mediation can be a wonderful tool that helps strengthen their ability to concentrate. Distractions are all around us, from the chime of our mobile devices to the advertisements that flood our newsfeed when we log onto social media. Distractions stop us from seeing reality as it is, and once we stop to pay attention, we start to realize what truly matters to our happiness.

Unlike those flashy and over the top performances you might see on TV, clinical hypnosis is actually simple. Hypnosis can be defined as a trance state of mind characterized by extreme relaxation, acute suggestibility, and heightened imagination. It's not that you are sleeping, but hypnosis is usually compared to daydreaming. The idea here is that your mind is fully alert and conscious, however, the stimuli surrounding you is not acute and turned out. Your mind is fully conscious, but most of the stimuli around you are tuned out. Your entire focus is intent on the subject at hand, excluding any other thought. It is all about focusing the mind, which is why it generally takes place in a quiet space. Preferably, you would have a room with dim lights, and if you wanted, gentle music could be playing in the background. That's another similarity it shares with meditation, which also calls for a quiet environment and perhaps some soft, gentle music playing in the background if you prefer.

A hypnotist will try to get you to focus your mind. A skilled hypnotist can help you create imaginary situations in your mind. Through hypnosis, you imagine your surroundings, and it feels like it's surreal, and these images are heightened as it engages your emotions. Imaginary situations can cause real sadness, fear, or happiness, and you may even jolt up from your seat if you are surprised or scared about something in your hypnosis. The hypnotist will walk you through relaxation exercises until you reach a state of focused relaxation. When you reach this state, it means your mind has arrived at the point where you are calmer, a lot more relaxed, and thus, open to suggestions. Once you're in the state, the hypnotist can guide you through several instructions or visualizations. Could you imagine what kind of power a manipulator might hold if they had the power to hypnotize too?

## What It Psychologically Means to Be Hypnotized

There is a theory called the *Altered State Theory*. This theory believes that through hypnosis, the mind is guided to a distinct state of consciousness. Like sleep, hypnosis is described as a distinct state of your brain. When you are in this state, the brain's process works differently, and you might not be aware of everything that is happening. According to hypnotism expert, Milton Erickson, people hypnotize themselves unknowingly on a daily basis. Psychiatrists trained in hypnosis focus primarily on the trance state of mind that brings in relaxation, calm, and focus. This is called deep hypnosis, and it is often related to the relaxed state of mind between sleep and wakefulness. In daily hypnosis practice, a hypnotist will have a session with you to understand your concerns, your ideas, and come up with suggestions. You approach these suggestions as if they were real. For example, if the hypnotist suggests that you drink a strawberry milkshake, you will taste the milkshake and feel the sensation of the drink going down your mouth and throat. This is 'playing pretend' but on a more intense level.

The second theory is called the *Non-State Theory*. In this theory, hypnosis is believed to be a combination of intense focus and some expectations about what it means to be hypnotized. According to this theory, the person could very well be aware of what is going on and playing along. With both theories, hypnosis is a process that is voluntary. For hypnotism to be effective, you have to be willing to listen to the hypnotist and willing to allow your mind to drift into that relaxed state. This is why a manipulator would need to gain a person's trust before they can pull off hypnotism without running the risk of looking suspicious.

## Hypnosis Frees Your Mind

It's not clear yet what makes someone more susceptible to hypnosis than others. Some researchers believe that it could have something to do with a person's brain anatomy. Hypnosis is believed to cause an increase in the brain's theta waves, which is linked to the brain's visualization and attention span. Hypnosis puts people in a more relaxed and inhibited state, and it is because they tune out any worries or doubts they usually have that prevents them from keeping their actions in check. It's like when you watch a movie or read a really good book. You're engrossed in the plot, and for a brief two to three hours, you forget about whatever it is that's worrying you- your job, your family, your projects, etc. You're focused on just what's on the screen or in the book. Hypnosis affects the way that your brain pays attention to certain things, and it supports the idea that your brain enters into a state of focused relaxation. This is when hypnotism is at its optimal.

This state of focused relaxation then allows the hypnotist (or manipulator if they know how to use this technique) to come in and influence a person's mind through a concept that is called *Top-Down Processing*. The human brain processes a lot of sensory data from the world around us. Our brain has to process and interpret the data we receive to better understand what is going on. In the *Top-Down Processing* approach, the top level of data is your memories and assumptions. This can have a big impact on what you perceive with your senses. When an experiment was done on two groups of people, one group drank wine that they were told was expensive. The other group drank wine and was told that it was a cheaper alternative. They were both the same wine, but the group that thought they were drinking the expensive one said it tasted better *because they expected it* to taste better. This also explains the placebo effect. If a doctor were to give you a pill and told you it was medicine, you would believe the doctor because you trusted them. The pill could be a piece of candy that did nothing for you, yet you would still claim to feel better because you expected to feel better.

Hypnotism only works when a person is open to suggestions. When you're in a state of focused relaxation, you are also highly suggestible. This is the point where the hypnotist tells you to do something, and you'll likely embrace that idea completely. But before you get worried that they can tell you to do anything you want (such as the ones you see on a stage hypnotists' performance- getting sensible adults doing funny things like jumping frogs), a hypnotist cannot get you to do anything you do not want to do. In this state of mind, a person's expectations would be tweaked, and the way they perceive the world around them could be changed.

## Hypnotism Is Not Fake?

No, it isn't. Although what you see on TV and magic shows probably is, since those are mainly for entertainment purposes. But *real hypnosis* is anything but fake, as we have already seen. It is a form of *psychotherapy*, a form of therapy where a person can be gently guided into a deep, relaxed state. When used in therapy, the therapist helps their patients to create the changes that they are looking for in their life by slowly reprogramming the mind through the power of suggestion. This is what manipulators do when they try to "suggest" that you do what they want but in a less devious way. The power of suggestion is an interesting concept. It was first researched by Faria, Bernheim, Liebeault, and the Nancy School. It begins with Father Abbe Faria, who started his research on hypnosis in India back in 1813. This Indo-Portuguese priest returned to Paris to continue his studies on hypnosis with Puysegur, and it was Faria that proposed the fact that it was not the power of the hypnotist neither magnetism that resulted in trance and healing, but instead, power was derived from within the mind of the person. The basis for clinical and theoretical work was Faria's approach in the French school known as the Nancy School, a hypnosis-centered psychotherapy school, also known as the *School of Suggestion.*
Founded by a French doctor named Ambroise-Auguste Leibeault, the Nancy School thinking was that hypnosis was a normal occurrence instigated by suggestion and not the effects of magnetism. Dr. Ambroise was considered the father of modern hypnotherapy, and he considered that hypnosis was psychological, disregarding theories of magnetism. He also studied the similarities between a trance state and a sleep state. From Leibeault, physician Hippolyte Bernheim became interested. A prominent neurologist, Bernheim observed Lieubault and eventually pursued hypnotism, abandoning medicine. Bernheim wrote about Leibeault's teachings in his own book *Suggestive Therapeutics*, offering it to the medical world as a form of science. To this day, Leibeault and Bernheim are considered the innovators of modern psychotherapy. The power of suggestion works so well for those who are able to open their

mind to the possibility because once you arrive in that trance-like state, you are able to block your mind off from the worries and the external distractions that plague you daily. A similar benefit to that of meditation. Professionally, hypnosis is always done in conjunction with other forms of psychotherapy treatments.

If a manipulator could coax others into a relaxed state, they can subtly influence them to change their minds. They know that once their victims are relaxed, suggestions are easily penetrated into the mind, and when combined with persuasion, it can be a very powerful force of change. An important key point to note here is that hypnosis is *only going to work when there is an element of trust*. Therefore, before you can even try this method, you need to get the person you are trying to influence to trust you. If they don't trust you, they are not going to listen to you. It is as simple as that.

## Is There A Difference Between Hypnosis, Persuasion, Influence, and Manipulation?

Yes, there is. Hypnosis is used to appeal to our subconscious mind. Hypnotism comes from a place that needs rapport, trust as well as a level of agreement and acceptance. Hypnosis, when administered and done correctly, will allow you to make suggestions to your subconscious mind. In a professional setting, hypnosis is used to influence without manipulating too. Influence is really tied to social standing or the relationship dynamic that you have with a person you want to influence. Influence often involves some form of authority or dominance over a person or a group, and this element is what moves them to have a presence or become the source of influence. For instance, a lecturer instructing their students or a judge giving an order are examples of influence. Hypnosis relies on communication to direct attention, seed ideas, and lead cognition. The aim is to lead a person into a state of altered perception.

Then we talk about influence and persuasion. Influence and persuasion are defined as the power to affect or change a person or situation, and this power to cause change is not a direct result of forcing them into making it happen. An influencer or persuader is an influential person in your life. There could be any number of individuals who are capable of coming into our lives and leaving such a deep impact that they influence us to become just a little bit better than we were before we met them. When we influence someone, it requires us to base it upon building a similar vision of the future. We need to share in that same excitement as the other party about reaching those goals and turning that vision into reality. In this way, influence differs vastly from manipulation, because there are false hope and breaking of promises that is taking place. You're not purposely deceiving them into believing in a vision that you have no intention of helping them fulfill. Persuasion and influence have the power to create positive change. With these two concepts, you are making careful observations about what works for them and what may not be in their best interest. While you're listening actively, you're still maintaining an open mind, and you're willing to share your own ideas about what you think might work for you and what you believe may not be in your best interest. This two-way communication process enables a bond of trust to form, something which can never happen when manipulation is taking place.

Manipulation is the social transaction that involves an attempt to get someone to see your point of view and to agree with what you do and what you say, and it's often in your favor. When it comes to manipulation, it often involves intent. Is the intent to find an agreement that cherishes both sides of values, or is it an attempt to find an agreement that fits in with your own line of interest? Manipulation seeks to take advantage of another person's vulnerable state. With hypnosis, persuasion, and influence, there is no underlying sinister intent. That only happens with manipulation. Manipulation doesn't take the time to justify or point out why your approach makes more sense and why the person you are trying to convince should follow it. Manipulation is bad if your underlying intentions are. As a concept, it is not inherently bad or good. There are positive forms of the manipulation taking place all around us already, except that we tend to refer to them as "influence" rather than manipulation. The term "manipulate," it leaves the impression that the other party is being forced into something against their will. Almost as if they didn't have a choice in the matter. When we use the term "influence" on the other hand, it leaves you with the impression that you're giving the other party options, and it is up to them at the end of the day to decide which direction they want to head towards. All of the above are still methods of coercing the individual to go in one direction or the other, but the only difference is manipulation is the most underhanded, devious, and sinister way of getting what you want. The biggest downside to manipulation is that relationships can fall apart and be destroyed, once people realize they have been manipulated.

Hypnosis may seem like it is complete and total mind control, another factor that sets it apart from manipulation. The truth is, however, that complete mind control is not possible, despite what hypnotists and performers who use this entertainment would like you to believe. A lot of people think that hypnosis is just used to make someone do something that is against their will, which is why a lot of people view hypnotism in a very negative light, plus it doesn't help that several movies portray hypnotism as an attempt to manipulate and control a person. Hypnosis cannot be used for mind control. Even the KGB and CIA have both experimented on the effects and uses of hypnotism in an attempt to create the perfect spy or assassin. There has been a lot of research on this but not a huge amount of proven success. Can someone hypnotize you to do something against your will? The general consensus and answer is *no they cannot*.

Hypnosis, at its very core, can be used to instill a series of feelings, images, or stories on one person and then encourage them to commit or do something that they would never otherwise consider. Manipulation uses *force, emotional blackmail, and threats* to get the same job done. Hypnosis can be used to encourage and promote a complete mind by reprogramming damaging thoughts and helping a person with a destructive attitude to great a specific plan. Manipulation doesn't care about what happens to you or how you feel. It is all about what the manipulator wants for themselves. Hypnosis can be persuasive, but it does not give control to the hypnotist. They do not have any control over your morality, mind, sense of being, or rationality.

## Hypnotizing Them to Say Yes With the ABS Technique

The most powerful hypnosis technique you could implement is the *power of your word choices*. But first, for hypnosis to work, it has to be based on a few principles. One of those principles is that the person you're trying to hypnotize must *want to listen to you*. If someone doesn't want to talk to you or listen to you in the first place, it is never going to work. They have to *want* to talk to you because only then will their mind be open and receptive to what you have to say. You could use all the most influential words you can think of, but if that person has already mentally shut themselves off to anything you have to say, your techniques are going to fall on deaf ears. The second principle is congruence. Your words need to be congruent with your actions. For example, when you're using those powerful, suggestive, and hypnotic words, you must project an air of confidence as you do.

The third principle is you need to speak clearly and distinctly when you do. You have to be specific about your word choices, and each sentence you say has to be for a purpose. The fourth principle is, you must know who your audience is. What you say has to be something they can easily accept and digest. It can't be a request that is too outrageous or alarming right away, because that is only going to increase their anxiety and they won't be listening to you. Your words have to be something that they can envision themselves doing. For example, *close your eyes for a minute. Pause your reading, close your eyes, and imagine a blue door*. That is an example of a suggestion that is easily acceptable and a suggestion you can easily envision in your mind. A blue door is easy enough to picture.

Now, we come to the words to use. Words have the power to create pictures in your mind and form associations and perceptions. The power words listen below each serves their own purpose and increases in power as they are combined the right way. Words that hypnotists use have a profound effect on hypnotic power. They can evoke a soothing quality, they can provoke anger, they can income calm and resilience. It's all about power play using words. One example of a powerful word is the word "***because.***" When you're trying to hypnotize someone, you might say something like this: *You are listening to me speak, you are listening to my voice, you can relax, and because you are relaxing, you feel more at ease because you are feeling comfortable, it helps you feel relaxed.* The word "***imagine***" is also another example of a powerful word choice since it invokes visions in the other person's mind. For example, here is what you might say if you were trying to hypnotize someone: *Imagine yourself walking towards the setting sun, sitting on a beach and listening to the waves. Imagine the sea caressing your feet as it reaches the shore. Imagine feeling realized and letting go of any worry.* Close your eyes and picture that sentence in your mind. Do you see how powerful word choices can be? Your words need to *tell* the other person what you would like them to do, but not in a manner that seems too bossy or demanding.

Hypnotic power words are designed to help you achieve three things and to do it all at one go. These three things are in a formula known as the ***ABS Technique.*** The repetition in the themes and the words you use will make others attentive and eat up your words because these words and phrases are daily words you'd use, but they are naturally engaging. The ***ABS Technique*** is a conversational method of hypnosis that focuses on three key areas:

- **A**bsorb Attention
- **B**ypass the Critical Factor
- **S**timulate the Unconscious

When someone is very comfortable around you and engaged in what you are telling them, you've got their attention. You've given these words an irresistible quality that enables you to bypass critical factors and allow your clients to feel more relaxed because of what you've said to them. It's an unconscious, natural reaction. It is imperative that you gain their *attention,* which is why *Absorb Attention* is the first point in this technique. If they are paying attention to you, they are going to be entranced as you carry on the conversation while employing the other two steps in this technique. With every spoken word, their body is responding the way you want them to- positively, calmly, listening to your suggestions, and having mental clarity. Keep in mind, it's not because they are controlling how they react, rather they are letting go of their inhibitions and their unconscious mind is fed with data.

Arrest their attention right from the start and make that your primary focus when you're trying to hypnotize them. The more attention they give you, the easier it is going to be to entrance them. To gain their attention, you must emit a state of positivity. This means that you need to start with positive energy from yourself. This is important because you want to bring out the best in others, and if you do not radiate positive energy, there's very little you can do for the person you're speaking to. Positive people are so easily able to command a room or a big crowd because there is something about them that draws everyone else's attention in their direction. It is a positive energy that they radiate. Your intention should begin with wanting to do the very best for your client. Be as energetic and positive as you can. Seek their consent, don't forget to do that. Ask them for permission to touch them on their shoulders during the induction before going into a trance. You need to make them feel comfortable in your presence, and if they are willing to let you touch them, that's a very positive sign already.

The next step in the **ABS Technique** is ***bypassing the critical factor***. This means you need to stop them from shutting down their minds to your suggestions. You need to bypass that mechanism so your message can slip right through. To do this, you need to gain their trust and make them comfortable. Initially, when you first meet the manipulator, they make you feel special. They make you trust them and let your guard down by making you feel comfortable in their presence. It is only when you start noticing the little signs that you realize something is not quite right. Make them look to you for the answers, and they will be under your spell.

Finally, the last step in the technique is ***stimulating the unconscious mind.*** To do this, *you* need to have an idea or direction that you would like the person to go to. This is where your language skills come into play. Here are other examples of powerful word choices:

- **Pretend** - It works along the same lines as the word ***imagine*** and produces the same desired effect: *Pretend that you are a great pianist and act as if you are going into hypnotism. Soon your mind forgets to pretend and start working on becoming a great pianist.* Words like imagine or pretend give the person you're talking to something to focus on, and this will start to stimulate their unconscious mind. An interesting fact about the unconscious mind is that it cannot distinguish between what is real and what is imagined. If you can imagine something vividly, your mind can be tricked into believing that it is real. This is how masterful hypnotists are able to seemingly hypnotize someone into doing what they want. When you use words like pretend or imagine, you're getting the listener to dive into their own minds and mentally rehearse the scenario in their head. They will imagine themselves doing what we ask, and if they can picture it, they'll be more receptive to the request.
- **More** - Invokes the idea of abundance in their mind, and abundance is something we all want. When we are introduced to the idea that we could have more of something, we immediately

seek it out. *The more you listen to my voice, the more you will feel relaxed, and you will soon forget your worries. The more you focus on your inner voice, the more comfortable you will feel with yourself.*

- **Every Time** - You're telling the person what is going to happen, without *insisting* that they do it. *Every time you breathe in, you will feel yourself going into a deeper state of comfort and relaxation. Every time you feel this way, you will go into a trance.* With this word selection, it is like you're indirectly telling them what will happen automatically. A reaction that can't be helped.
- **What Was It Like** - This is another phrase that invokes imagery in their minds. *Think about what it was like when you felt happy. What did you feel? How did you feel physically and mentally?* These words all seem ordinary but placed in the right context power comes out when you know how to use them. The more vivid the image is in their mind, the greater your chances of subtle hypnotizing them into saying yes to your request.
- **You** - Using the word "you" in place of their name can be incredibly hypnotic. Using the person's name too often can be a little bit awkward and uncomfortable if you don't know them all that well. Plus, using their name too often can make the conversation feel unnatural. When you use the word "you," it makes it much easier for them to picture themselves in whatever the scenario you ask them to imagine. It makes them feel like the focus of the conversation is about them when you emphasize the word "you." Once they believe that the conversation is about them, their interest immediately goes up. Before they know it, they'll find themselves hanging onto your every word.

# CONCLUSION

Thank you for making it through to the end of *Manipulation for Beginners*, and let's hope it was informative and able to provide you with all of the tools you need to achieve your goals whatever they may be.

Behind the charming smile and friendly persona, a person's true intentions might not be what they seem. But manipulation is not all bad, and it can be used for both good and evil, and whatever the outcome is will depend entirely on your intention. *It is your intention that will make the difference* between whether you're manipulative or persuasive. Understanding these fundamentals of manipulation will give you a better insight into the way the human mind works. Not only will you be able to use these techniques to influence the people around you, but you will be able to discern when *someone else may be using these tactics on you.*

Whether we like it or not, manipulation happens all around us every day. Some people choose to do it, and some do it without realizing how manipulative their actions and words are. By making it to the end of this book, you're no longer in the latter category. Now that you're off to a good start at understanding what manipulation is all about, how are you going to use everything you just learned?

Finally, if you found this book useful in any way, a review on Amazon is always appreciated!

# DESCRIPTION

*If you had the ability to influence people into doing anything you want, would you do it?*
The world would be a much happier place if everyone could do what we wanted them to, right? We often wished we could get people to do what we want, when we wanted them to. But what if you knew *there was a way* to do that? With a little subtle manipulation and persuasion?
Manipulation. It has a bad reputation that goes along with it. But truth be told, manipulation is only bad *because* of what we choose to do with it. Manipulation could be used for both good and evil. Like everything else, it is about balance and the right way to use these techniques.
It is all about mind games and mental control. When you understand how the human mind works, you'll realize how easily we can be persuaded. Manipulation, in a way, gives you the ability to control the actions and thoughts of another. There are several skills involved in pulling this off effectively, but that is why you're here. To learn everything that you need to introduce you to the world of manipulation.
To the manipulator, there is power to be gained when you learn how to control the people around you. They are constantly on the lookout for ways they can gain the upper hand over the people around them. Getting people to do what you want is a skill that can be developed. Once you understand the way manipulation works, it can prove to be a useful skill when you need it. In *Manipulation for Beginners*, these are the basics you will cover:
- An introduction into the world of manipulation and gaslighting
- The signs that *you* could be a victim of gaslighting
- Understanding who the three-major manipulative personality group are
- How to define and understand the difference between manipulation and persuasion
- Common psychological tricks used to persuade anyone, no matter who they are
- The key phrases to winning people over
- Manipulative tactics that tug at your emotional heartstrings
- Why the silent treatment is a classic but dangerous manipulative move
- How to make anyone agree *when* you want them to
- Why people choose to say no and foolproof ways to change their mind
- How to put anyone under your spell through conversational-hypnosis
- Why hypnotism is not fake and how it can free your mind
- Introducing the ABS Technique to hypnotizing anyone

The human mind is a remarkable domain, and when you understand how it works, you can get anyone to do anything, and they wouldn't even know why. If you could learn to manipulate and persuade the people around you, it is going to change your relationships and put you in a position of power when you are the one dominating and directing the conversational flow. How do you get people to say yes to you? By being the one in control, and this is where your first step begins. Are you ready to stay one step ahead of everyone else?

# DARK PSYCHOLOGY SECRETS

*Learn The Secrets Of The Mind And Control Your Life With Persuasion, Manipulation, And Emotional Intelligence*

**Marisa Leary**

© Copyright 2020 by Marisa Leary. All right reserved.
The work contained herein has been produced with the intent to provide relevant knowledge and information on the topic on the topic described in the title for entertainment purposes only. While the author has gone to every extent to furnish up to date and true information, no claims can be made as to its accuracy or validity as the author has made no claims to be an expert on this topic. Notwithstanding, the reader is asked to do their own research and consult any subject matter experts they deem necessary to ensure the quality and accuracy of the material presented herein.

This statement is legally binding as deemed by the Committee of Publishers Association and the American Bar Association for the territory of the United States. Other jurisdictions may apply their own legal statutes. Any reproduction, transmission or copying of this material contained in this work without the express written consent of the copyright holder shall be deemed as a copyright violation as per the current legislation in force on the date of publishing and subsequent time thereafter. All additional works derived from this material may be claimed by the holder of this copyright.

The data, depictions, events, descriptions and all other information forthwith are considered to be true, fair and accurate unless the work is expressly described as a work of fiction. Regardless of the nature of this work, the Publisher is exempt from any responsibility of actions taken by the reader in conjunction with this work. The Publisher acknowledges that the reader acts of their own accord and releases the author and Publisher of any responsibility for the observance of tips, advice, counsel, strategies and techniques that may be offered in this volume.

# INTRODUCTION

Congratulations on purchasing *Dark Psychology Secrets,* and thank you for choosing this book to begin your study of dark psychology.

This book is everything you need to get started on the path to understanding dark psychology. This book is designed to be user-friendly so that you move seamlessly from foundational concepts into the more complicated and nuanced aspects of this topic. You will learn how to take the basics and recognize them, understand where dark psychology can go too far, and develop the skills needed to apply it thoughtfully in your own life, if you dare. If you have ever wondered why success comes so easily to those in power, you will know by the end of this book. If you have ever wondered why victims fall prey so easily to well-known predators, you will know by the end of this book. And if you have ever wondered how to enjoy the kind of success enjoyed by the powerful elite, you will get the chance to taste that same success with just a little study and practice. This is your ultimate guide. The secrets are waiting in this book, just for you, and it is the author's sincere hope that you will finish the book satisfied that you are now an expert in the world of dark psychology.

There are plenty of books on dark psychology on the market, so thank you for trusting this one to be your guide. Every effort was made to ensure that it creates a lasting impact on your understanding and use of dark psychology practices. Please enjoy!

# CHAPTER 1
*What Is Dark Psychology?*

You have begun your journey into dark psychology, and the most obvious first step is to understand what it is. The answer is both simple and complicated, so feel free to return to this opening chapter to remind yourself of the basic foundation of what dark psychology is. Grapple with the definition and use it as a way to challenge your understanding of the concept as this book delves deeper into its nuances.

## Dark Psychology Basics

In its purest definition, dark psychology is the innate human ability to prey upon others, with or without a clear motivation. It acknowledges that within every human being is the capability to act upon these inclinations to victimize and engage in predatory behavior. This predatory behavior manifests itself as strategic manipulation and coercion that often goes unnoticed by the victim.

The most common form of dark psychology manifests itself as minor forms of aggression and behaviors. A reaction to a negative stimulus can cause an immediate desire to perform harm or to engage in violent retaliation. In other words, if someone has hurt you in some way, the thought may cross your mind to hit them. You don't necessarily act on the thought, but it's still there. This is entirely human. Everyone has the basic requirements of dark psychology within them.

This is also a uniquely human phenomenon because it strays from the basic instincts common to most other living things. Violence in the animal world serves the purpose of securing a territory, securing reproductive capabilities, or pure survival. Humans, on the other hand, can engage in not only physical violence but also emotional violence in order to inflict pain on someone. This can come from a large range of motivations outside of territory, reproduction, or survival, or it can have no motivation at all. This is why dark psychology requires careful study because it takes a look into a much darker side of the human condition.

When studying dark psychology, it is essential to anchor the idea that we are all capable of utilizing dark psychology, but the ways in which it is used vary from person to person. In other words, it falls along a spectrum that can range from only thoughts of predatory behavior to actualized predatory behavior that is incredibly violent and without a clear motive. So, in that sense, dark psychology is not necessarily inherently evil or even deplorable. It is a natural part of being human. The danger lies in where a person falls along this spectrum and whether their decisions can be connected to motivations or not.

Another part of understanding this topic is learning that dark psychology is in constant use. Whether you are conscious of it or not is different. For example, dark psychology has and always will play a role in advertising practices. At its heart, advertising is seeking to make consumers the "victims" of their sales tactics, even if what is being sold has no direct impact on someone's basic human needs. There is no evolutionary justification for why you may want a new phone, but dark psychology tactics can be used to convince you otherwise. Word choice, product placement, colors, and catchphrases can all be used to sway you to want a product regardless of its utility.

Now that you are beginning to understand the ubiquitous qualities of dark psychology, you may be in a panic. You may even be having regrets about a recent purchase you made or a response you gave to someone who used dark psychology to draw you in. Stop right there because it is not worth giving yourself a headache over what is done. Instead, take this moment as an opportunity to see that learning about dark psychology can also give you power over dark psychology. Rather than living in a world where you are unconsciously tempted into all manner of behaviors and decisions, you will now live in a world where you are self-aware and can combat the more deviant aspects of dark psychology.

Dark psychology divides itself very easily into two categories: the perpetrator and the victim. These two categories can be made up of individuals or multiple individuals, but both must be represented in order for dark psychology to be in action. The whole point is to gain control over another's behavior, so at least two people must be involved. The perpetrator is, of course, the person or people who are actively using dark psychological tactics. The perpetrator most often has one clear goal, and that is to satisfy something they want. They may want the victim to feel belittled, friendless, unsuccessful, or simply want them to be in physical pain. To secure what they want, they will use a variety of manipulation tactics to create the desired result. You will learn more about the specifics of these tactics in a future chapter, but for now, understand that there are recognizable tools used by perpetrators to get what they want from their victims. If successful, the perpetrator will have manipulated and coerced the victim into committing the desired behaviors or reactions. A successful perpetrator will often return to the same victim and fine-tune their tactics over time to master the art of dark psychology.

Another way to think of it is that the perpetrator is controlling your mind. They are observing you, watching for what makes you behave in certain ways, and then using those triggers to generate the desired response. It is calculating and specific. This is the characteristic of dark psychology that steps beyond the natural angry responses we may have and becomes a deeply intentional act that can stray into criminal and deviant behavior. The victim can be anyone, as long as the victim is the subject of the perpetrator's actions. The victim is most often unaware of how dark psychology is being used against them. They may not even see the perpetrator as someone "bad." Instead, they believe that their responses are born of their own free decisions. What they are unaware of is how everything they do and say is as the perpetrator predicted. The perpetrator is often masterful at making the victim feel that they chose the behavior rather than believing that they were manipulated. The victim may even defend and support the perpetrator if the perpetrator is strong enough in the tactics of dark psychology. This is where dark psychology becomes most dangerous because it is literally morphing the mind of the victim. It is not a relatively harmless sales strategy but is true mind control and manipulation.

Do not be entirely misled by the use of the word victim. It has a negative implication, but that does not mean it is always negative to be a victim or to be a perpetrator. It is inevitable that dark psychology tactics will be used on you and by you. What is most significant is the motivation. For example, you may have a friend you know is in the throes of an abusive relationship. It is entirely valid to use what you know about them and their personality to manipulate them into seeing the abuse they are suffering. While no one likes to engage in or be the victim of manipulation, there are relevant times to put dark psychology to use.

### A Brief History of Dark Psychology

If you were to attempt to do some initial research on the history of dark psychology, you would come up with woefully few results. That is because most psychological experiments that deal with factors related to dark psychology will go by other names. Some common ones would be social psychology or social experiments. Below you will find two experiments that ventured into the realms of dark psychology as well as a psychologist who was a pioneer for the kinds of social experiments in use today. Studies and psychologists such as these provide another source of validation for the permeation and prevalence of dark psychology within humanity.

The first study of interest was performed by Stanley Milgram. In his study, subjects were told to sit at a panel, which had a microphone, speaker, and a labeled dial. They were to listen to a subject answer a series of questions. The subjects were at the panel, and the responders were supposedly in another room. Subjects were unable to see the responder, but they were able to hear all of their responses and other sounds over the speaker. The responders, of course, never received a shock but were simply recordings of a person's voice played for the subjects. Subjects were told the dial was to be used to deliver an electric shock to the responder if they gave an incorrect response to a question. The dial was labeled with varying degrees of pain inflicted, including the highest label of "fatal." The subjects who sat at the panel would deliver these shocks as directed by a person in the room with them. This person had a white lab coat on but did not present any other credentials. If the subject hesitated to increase the shock as the responder answered more questions incorrectly, the person in the white lab coat would follow a script of responses that all ultimately told the subject they had no choice and that it had to be done.

The results of this experiment were shocking, but they show very clearly the power of dark psychology at work. The subject who was told to deliver the shocks continued to increase the severity of pain, even to the "fatal" level, and even while hearing pre-recorded screams coming from the responder. Sixty-five percent of subjects did not stop at the "fatal" level, and even those who did refuse to continue simply left after the experience and in no way showed concern over the fate of the responder they were shocked.

What this experiment clearly illustrates is twofold. First, it validates that we are all capable of performing acts we may deem "immoral" or "wrong" in the right circumstances. Second, it illustrates the dangers of positions of authority. Although the person with the lab coat was unknown to the subject, the lab coat gave the wearer a kind of authority, which the subject responded to, even against their better judgment or moral values. Normal human beings were willing to engage in acts of torture because they trusted in that authority, even if it meant killing an unknown person. Dark psychology can be used to terrible effect when utilized by the wrong individuals, especially those entrusted with power.

The second experiment was designed by Philip Zimbardo and was called the Stanford Prison Experiment. The goal of the study was to perfectly simulate the conditions of prison. Subjects were divided into two groups, prison guards and inmates. They were given quarters that were designed to mimic a prison in every way possible, a true recreation of the prison environment. After that, the subjects were left to operate in their roles as they saw fit without any outside direction or interference. The study was designed to last for a two-week period, but it had to be shut down after only six days. Within those six days, the prison guards had already begun to engage in sadistic and manipulative ways towards the prisoners. Of course, no one expected that they would fall so easily into these patterns of behavior, and none wanted to acknowledge that the circumstances manipulated them into making decisions uncharacteristic of their personalities and personal morals.

This experiment is another prime example of dark psychology in action. All it took was the appropriate stimulus for individuals to engage in dangerous and exploitative behavior. The subjects entered as peers, but the labels they were given, one with innate authority and one without, meant that they changed as people. This experiment has a deeper implication that goes beyond an abuse of power. This study was a group study rather than an individual study. That means that, regardless of who initiated the negative behavior towards the prisoners, the rest of the prison guards went along with it and even actively participated in it.

Many of those individuals may protest their innocence, but their inaction showed acceptance of the deviant behavior coming from someone in a position of authority.

There is one psychologist who played a pivotal role in launching the idea of social psychology and experimentation. His name was John Broadus Watson. He was a proponent of using direct observation of behaviors to help understand their stimuli. He engaged in many experiments that utilized rats in order to make conjectures about how humans would respond in similar circumstances.

Watson realized that connecting a stimulus to a response meant that you could predict how a subject would respond. This meant whoever controlled the stimulus essentially controlled the subject. The subject's response would be a direct result of that stimulus and not of the subject's individual choice. This simple connection between cause and effect is what makes dark psychology so successful and so potentially insidious. If someone already knows what to do to force you into a particular decision, you have been robbed of free will without ever noticing it was gone.

The scientific application of social psychology was not Watson's only interest. When he was ousted from the academic world, he applied his knowledge to the government and private sector, specifically the military and advertising. With the military, he helped design some of the first aptitude tests to evaluate which soldiers would be best for serving in particular positions. These types of tests are still in use today. With advertising, he helped pioneer sales tactics that are also still in use today. It all started with the foundational element of social experiments: observation. He masqueraded as a salesperson in order to observe the average consumer and to reach conclusions on what would motivate them to buy. This led to him recognizing the importance of having a target demographic. A product with a target demographic will be able to customize its slogans to suit the tastes of that part of the population. For example, a new mother will be motivated to buy products that mention safety. He also discovered the immense power of celebrity endorsement. People are psychologically motivated by public figures they admire, so attaching that power to a product promotes sales.

The bottom line of all of his experiments and creations can be summed up in the term dark psychology. If you know how a person will react, that means that you hold their behavior in your hand. With a simple stimulus, you can generate nearly any response you desire. With the power of authority, the power of the stimulus is also increased. Although human beings like to flatter themselves that they are capable of behaving as free-thinking individuals at all times, dark psychology, and these historical experiments, prove otherwise. Humanity has within it the ability to be manipulated and coerced even into torturing another unknown human being. This means that we must learn to be wary of how dark psychology may be shaping our own behavior and also how we can use dark psychology to avoid victimization by the many perpetrators in our midst.

# CHAPTER 2
*Characteristics Of Dark Psychology*

Now that you have begun to grasp the basic concept of dark psychology, here is a deeper dive into its key characteristics. This is not an exhaustive list because a future chapter will take a closer look at these characteristics. Consider this an overview of some of the details of dark psychology. This is another good chapter to revisit, especially when you are looking to gauge whether someone is guilty of using dark psychology against you. It is also another chapter worth revisiting when you want to understand if you are diving too deeply into dark psychology. There is a fine line between dark psychology that has good intentions and dark psychology that is approaching evil. This is a chapter that can help you decipher and evaluate your own emotions before engaging in unnecessarily risky or morally repugnant behaviors.

## The Dark Triad

The Dark Triad is a common term used in dark psychology. Although the next chapter will deal with some key terms in dark psychology, it is necessary to have a beginning understanding of this term to truly understand the key points that make someone likely to use dark psychology. The Dark Triad is a hotly contested subject within dark psychology since the term was created only within this century. This means that there is likely much more research to be completed in order to truly understand what each of these terms means and how they manifest themselves in those who practice dark psychology. If you are looking to understand this concept from a different perspective, you may also consider looking into the light triad. It is intended to show the alternative sides of each part of the dark triad. Be sure to look at the explanation of the light triad in the following chapter to learn more.

The term **Dark Triad** is used to describe a trio of personality types that are known to engage in behaviors related to dark psychology. There have been some suggestions for a fourth, but these three are the most commonly discussed. These personality types have components that can overlap. Someone who uses dark psychology may fit into one of these categories. They may fit into a combination of two of these personality types. They may also fit into all three, which means they would be among the most deviant and dangerous individuals you could encounter. Whatever the case may be, if you become aware of someone who fits into one of these categories, you would do well to be on your guard when around them. Regardless of which category they fall into, they can pose a danger to you either emotionally or physically. Use this information to gain a deeper understanding of how they may act and why.

The first personality type of the Dark Triad is a narcissist. Many people are familiar with the term narcissism, but not many people are as familiar with a true narcissistic personality. A true narcissist goes beyond someone who is simply self-interested. True narcissism is so pervasive within these individuals that they cannot act outside of its constraints. They are made to be a narcissist and cannot see another way.

A **narcissist** believes with every fiber of their being that they are the most important person on earth. They are so completely drawn into this feeling that they are often blind to the needs and wants of others. They will always and in any situation center their needs over those of others, regardless of the consequences. This does not come from a choice, necessarily, but is it the product of their belief system. Their belief system has dictated that they are the center of everything, and it would not only be ill-advised but nearly impossible to convince a narcissist that their belief is wrong.

True narcissists often have intense and overpowering personalities in social settings. They tend to self-aggrandize and exaggerate in such a way that benefits themselves and no one else. If they are telling a story, they will be the hero of that story every time. This is not just self-delusion. They truly believe that they are the best of the best, that no one can beat them in any way. Although many will see that this is an act, those susceptible to and unaware of dark psychology tactics may easily become the victim of a narcissist. From a certain perspective, a narcissist may be a very charismatic and appealing figure. After all, their lies will paint them as the epitome of humanity, someone who is not only desirable but enviable. This can have a magnetic draw for those who may wish they were as confident and self-assured as the narcissist.

A final trait of narcissists is the unending need for attention. They will always place themselves at the center of any event and feel an overpowering need to be the focus of all the attention. Their ultimate desire is to be centerstage while everyone watches them in awe, and they will constantly seek to have an audience to watch them as they perform. Of course, their performances will feature them as the dominant figure and will often include others only if they increase the desirability of the narcissist or make them a more enviable figure.

When you combine all of these traits, a narcissist can be a nefarious individual if someone is naively drawn into their performance and actually believes what they say. Since most narcissists are pathological liars and exaggerators, a victim could find themselves falling for a person who quite literally does not exist. However, the narcissist can be such a convincing performer that the victim will be in denial for a long time and may even be the narcissist's top defender. If the victim has no reason to doubt the narcissist, they will, of course, support them. The narcissist is first and foremost an exceptional liar and performer, and many who perhaps suffer low self-esteem will be blindly drawn into this fantasy person. After all, who wouldn't want to be the narcissist? If only their lies were true.

The second personality type is related to the first but is lacking in showmanship. This is called Machiavellianism. While narcissists use lies to uplift themselves, a Machiavellian will use lies for personal gain. This eliminates the performative nature of the lies and can make them harder to detect.

**Machiavellianism** is the use of strategic deception and manipulation. This means a Machiavellian will use their words not to build themselves up but to trick you into becoming their performer. They will convince you to perform whatever they think will benefit them. They do not care how they achieve this result, only that they achieve it. They are goal-oriented at all times, which can make them vicious when they fully engage their powers.

Strategic deception is essentially lying with a purpose and lying in such a way that the listener will not know they are being lied to. Machiavellians are expert liars who will talk you in circles until you are so utterly lost in their lies that you cannot see where the lie began. Unlike narcissists, Machiavellians' lies are not about boosting their self-image. They have lied with clear intent and with a clear design for what they want to achieve. Strategic planning is the guiding principle behind their lies, so they will have formulated a clear plan before inflicting these lies on their victim. They will not jeopardize their goal with a poor lie but will use careful preparation to lure their victim.

Strategic manipulation is another trait of a Machiavellian. Strategic manipulation means they not only use their words to create believable lies, but also that they use those lies to manipulate you into certain behaviors. Their lies do not stop at believability. Instead, their lies are the catalysts for the behaviors they want you to perform. The Machiavellian has a deep understanding of the cause and effect relationship discussed in the first chapter. This is what makes them such masterful manipulators. They know in advance and after careful study exactly what to do and say to make their lies believable and to make them actionable. You will become their puppet as they pull the invisible strings to get you to do anything, while you remain blissfully unaware.

Machiavellians can be even harder to detect than narcissists because their motives may not be as clear. While it is easier to spot a narcissist because they direct everything to themselves, Machiavellians are much more subtle. They are not in the business of centering themselves but instead lie to achieve any number of motives. Unless you have a deep insight into their motivations, you may not be able to detect a Machiavellian at work. Their design may only become evident after it is too late. That is how intensely talented they are at deception and manipulation. You could be in their power before you would even know what happened. You could also be in a position where you could not fight the consequences of what the Machiavellian set in motion. After all, although the Machiavellian manipulated you, you still engaged in the action. You could argue that you did not do it freely or understand the consequences, but, depending on the situation, it can be impossible to fight back once a Machiavellian has reached their goal. They can always argue that you had a choice, and you chose to do as they desired.

The final personality type in the Dark Triad is psychopaths. Unlike narcissists and Machiavellians, psychopaths do not always have a clear design in mind or a clear focus to motivate their behaviors. This makes them highly unpredictable and nefarious. It has also made them the subject of massive amounts of study, speculation, and intrigue. You could even call them fascinating, although it would be a morbid fascination. It is difficult for someone who lies outside the realm of psychopathy to fully understand how and why they behave as they do. It is reminiscent of the phrase it's like a train wreck you see coming: you can't look away, even if it would be wiser to do so.

**Psychopaths** are characterized by their impulsive behavior and the absence of empathy. However, within the Dark Triad, psychopath refers merely to a personality type, not to a clinical diagnosis of psychopathy. In other words, a psychopathic personality may display some psychopathic traits but not to the extent that a clinical psychologist would diagnose them as a psychopath. For the sake of this text, they will be referred to as psychopaths, but understand that there is a difference between someone who is diagnosed versus someone who shows traits.

A psychopath's impulsivity makes them highly unpredictable and drastically different from a Machiavellian or a narcissist. The narcissists focus their decisions on themselves. The Machiavellians focus on manipulating those around them. Psychopaths may not have any clear motivation besides the fact that they enjoy witnessing chaos or pain. Their actions do not stem from careful study or strategy. If they want something, they go for it instantaneously, without prior warning. This can be both beneficial and detrimental to the psychopath. The complete lack of planning can mean it's much easier for the psychopath to move undetected. You cannot connect their behavior to any motives, other than they wanted to do it. However, impulsivity also equates to higher risk. It is possible that the lack of planning means they are sloppy. This sloppiness could mean them risking detection more often. Either way, impulsivity is dangerous in someone who engages in dark psychology. Predictability means safety. Psychopaths defy that safety.

The most sinister quality of a psychopath is the absence of empathy. They do not and cannot place themselves in someone else's perspective. They are blithely unaware of how their actions may affect the feelings of others and do not have an understanding of many human emotions. This means that they are more likely to behave in violent ways. Violence does not phase them because someone else's pain causes no sympathetic reaction in their own feelings. They could hear someone's screams and tears and be completely unmoved. They may even enjoy it because they do not understand normal human emotional reactions. They have no concept of what it means to cause someone else pain. What is even worse, they do not care. They cannot grasp what it means to care.

The combination of impulsivity and a lack of empathy makes psychopaths perhaps the most sinister of the three personality types. They move through life as they see fit, when they see fit, with complete disregard for the feelings of others. Feelings quite literally do not matter to them, which makes them most likely to become violent or to engage in risky criminal behavior. They do not see how these behaviors are objectionable because they do not see outside their own impulsive desires.

Psychopaths are most closely related to Machiavellians because of their tendency to manipulate to suit themselves, while narcissists are completely self-centered. However, there is a possibility that all of these personality types may be found in one person for a combination of two.

A narcissist with Machiavellian tendencies will be characterized by self-importance but also by manipulative behaviors. Rather than limit their lies to those that build their self-image, they will both exaggerate to elevate themselves and to manipulate those around them into behaving in certain ways. These two personality types working in conjunction characterize many of those who hold positions of power. Individuals are drawn to the appeal of the narcissist and are kept in control by the manipulation of the Machiavellian. Some may even describe this combination as charming because the person clearly works to benefit themselves but will stroke your own ego enough to coerce you into behaving in all sorts of ways. They are self-centered, but their lies can make you believe that they are thinking only of you. This is a tempting combination for those who may be psychologically vulnerable.

A narcissist with psychopathic tendencies will still be self-important but will also engage in risk-taking behavior that ignores the needs of others. This personality combination is less likely to be appealing to others because a narcissistic psychopath will not be able to clearly understand others' feelings. However, they will still be a pathological liar. This kind of individual will often come across as callous and unfeeling. That does not mean they cannot be dangerous to others. There are those who will fall prey to the charisma of the narcissistic side of their personality and become complicit in their psychopathic behaviors because they trust the narcissist. If someone were to believe their persona, they could be easily tempted into justifying the person's illicit behaviors.

A Machiavellian with psychopathic tendencies is perhaps one of the most dangerous personality combinations. Although psychopaths do not understand emotion, the calculating manipulation of a Machiavellian may help them learn to mimic these emotions. They will mimic emotions in order to create a desired response. This, combined with extreme impulsivity, means that Machiavellian psychopaths are very difficult to detect. Think of them as chameleons. They understand that they are not emotionally made like other people, and so they learn to put on whatever emotional response necessary to elicit a desirable behavior in their victim. It is a disconcerting conglomeration of personality traits. They may not be as appealing as a narcissist, but they will still be able to use performative manipulation that is convincing and motivating for the victim.

It is possible to have an individual who shows traits characteristic of all three personality types. This type of individual would be towards the darkest end of the dark psychology spectrum. First, they would be an exceptional performer who is utterly convinced of their own superiority. Second, they will use their performances to draw in and manipulate everyone around them. Their motives will be entirely selfish, and their means will be without limitations. Finally, they will engage all of these powerful traits to create chaos whenever and however they desire, all while completely ignoring the impact of their decisions and manipulations. In short, they live solely to control others to make themselves feel good. Their lack of empathy also means they do not fall prey to their own feelings or the feelings of others. They are emotionally flat and will only use emotion as a manipulation tactic or as a way to gain even more attention. If you become a victim of someone who falls into this category, you will have an incredibly difficult time seeing and understanding how you became the prey of such a predator. It could take months or even years of reflection to fully understand the ways in which they have controlled your life decisions and your emotional responses. That being said, it is not your fault if you find yourself a victim of one are all of these personalities. They are the product of the darker side of humanity, and the best you can do is to educate yourself further, so you do not become a victim again in the future. It is as much human to have characteristics of dark psychology as it is to be a victim of dark psychology.

Other Characteristics

Although many practitioners of dark psychology will have strong connections to a personality type in the Dark Triad, that is not always the case. There are a number of traits that are somewhat similar to these three, but they are still noteworthy in your study of dark psychology.

A related but less prevalent form of narcissism is egoism. **Egoism** is also self-centered but is more about the benefits the individual enjoys. They want things to go their way and have no concern about possible effects. They want to bask in the glory of something that makes them happy, and that is the only bottom line.

Another dark psychology trait is moral disengagement. This would be most directly connected to psychopathy. **Moral disengagement** means the individual can compartmentalize their feelings and set aside their personal morals when making a decision or taking action. While a psychopath has no choice in whether they can understand feelings, someone who uses moral disengagement plans to set aside their morals in order to act like a psychopath might act. In other words, they can choose to ignore their feelings of guilt and empathy. They can then reengage their morals after committing whatever act went against those morals and behave and react morally in other situations. This is a tricky character trait because it means someone could be perceived as more humane than a psychopath, yet they are almost worse because they have an innate understanding of empathy. They simply choose to set it aside.

The next trait is psychological entitlement. This would be most closely related to narcissism. **Psychological entitlement** is the deep belief that the individual is deserving of something above all others. They are like a narcissist because they are immersed in the belief that they are the best or the most deserving person. Unlike a narcissist, however, they are not about performance but are about benefits. They feel they deserve whatever is best because their merits surpass all others. This is a firmly held belief and not something the individual may be conscious of.

Spitefulness is another potential trait within dark psychology. It can be connected to both Machiavellianism and psychopathy. **Spitefulness** can be summed up by the word revenge. This type of individual is motivated by a need to retaliate. This can manifest as violent behaviors. What makes this trait so dangerous is that it is so all-consuming that the individual will do whatever it takes to achieve their revenge, even if they harm themselves in the process. This makes them somewhat Machiavellian because they are centered on a clear goal, but it also makes them psychopathic because they engage in any behavior regardless of consequences to others or themselves. It is an unfeeling trait.

Self-interest can also characterize dark psychology. It is connected to narcissism and Machiavellianism. **Self-interest** is what it sounds like: a desire to benefit oneself. It most often includes behaviors that will enhance a person's wealth or social status. It is similar to narcissism because it is entirely focused on the individual. It is like Machiavellianism in that it has a clear goal. Individuals who display this characteristic are more easily detected because of the clear motivations for the person's behaviors.

One of the most disturbing characteristics of dark psychology is sadism. It is most closely connected to psychopathy. **Sadism** is the desire to cause harm because of the satisfaction that it brings. This harm can be physical or emotional. What is most concerning about this trait is that the perpetrator truly achieves pleasure or enjoyment from witnessing the harm inflicted on the victim. This connects to psychopathy because it shows a lack of innate empathy. The victim's feelings are only of consequence because they bring satisfaction to the perpetrator.

Use these characteristics to understand how dark psychology may be at work in your own life, and use it to understand how to analyze and break free. Once you truly understand, dark psychology will no longer be a source of fear but a source of freedom.

# CHAPTER 3
## *Dark Psychology Terms Explained*

This chapter is meant to serve as a reference guide for you not only as you read this text but also as you need to return to it to refresh yourself on some of the key terms in the field. You will notice that there is some overlap between terms in this chapter and terms explained in other chapters. That is to enable you to have one location to return to if you only need a quick reminder rather than a full reread of an entire chapter. Please consider this chapter as one of the best tools in this text because it summarizes more succinctly the terms you will need to navigate dark psychology knowledgeably. It is also a perfect way to introduce a friend to some of the concepts you are studying. Let them take a peek and see if this text could become their guide as well.

### Basic Dark Psychology Terms

**Arsonist:** An arsonist is an individual who expresses not just a fascination with but an obsession with setting fires. An arsonist can be related to dark psychology because they are engaging in a behavior, which most often is done for their benefit, sometimes even pleasure, and is done at great cost to others. There is a predator, and there is a victim. What is less present in an arsonist is the components of manipulation and control. It could be said that an arsonist is seeking to manipulate and control the authorities and takes pride in the fact that they can get away with it. An arsonist's relationship to dark psychology would need to be analyzed on a case-by-case basis.

**Brainwashing:** Brainwashing is the systematic and methodical process of a victim fully believing in the power of the predator. The victim may not even acknowledge to themselves or others that they are being controlled. They will be wrapped up in the delusion that they are safer with the predator and must stay with the predator at all costs. It is characterized by many dark psychology practices, such as fatigue inducement, starvation, social-isolation, and more. It is also commonly used in organizations of people, such as cults. Its results can be notoriously difficult to reverse. Victims may spend decades continuing to believe that the perpetrator is still trustworthy.

**Choice restriction:** Choice restriction is an act in which the predator provides the victim with a series of choices but omits the choice they do not want the victim to make. In this way, the victim feels as though they are controlling their choices, but the reality is the choice that is undesirable for the predator is completely absent. It creates a delusional sense of power for the victim and makes it much harder to see the predator's manipulation. The victim will defend themselves by arguing that they always had a choice when the truth is they only had the choices the predator allowed.

**Dark Continuum:** The Dark Continuum is a spectrum of behavior that can be connected to dark psychology. This continuum encompasses all kinds of deviant and predatory behavior. It has a range that can go from purposeful, planned actions to wanton chaos. It can also go from mere thoughts of victimization to impulsive, violent, criminal acts. A person can travel along this spectrum at different points in their life according to how deeply they dive into dark psychology and how actively they work to use it on a daily basis. It is most likely that the majority of people will stay relatively low on the spectrum and not progress to its most devious end.

**Dark Factor:** Dark Factor is the amount of potential someone has to not only possess traits related to dark psychology but to put those traits into action on a regular basis. Someone's Dark Factor could be increased by life experiences, such as trauma during formative years or an unstable and unhealthy upbringing. These, combined with perhaps a personality type within the Dark Triad, will increase the amount of Dark Factor a person is likely to have. It is easy to say that someone has a large amount of Dark Factor because of circumstances out of their control, but that does not guarantee they will act on them. Be careful to avoid assumptions based on these indicators.

**Dark psychology:** This term encompasses the concept that every human has within them the innate ability to victimize another for no clear evolutionary purpose. The most easily identifiable characteristic of dark psychology is a desire to manipulate and control others for a variety of motivations, including physical, emotional, and psychological desires. Some would sum it up as mind control. However, it is a powerful human characteristic, which everyone is born with, but not all choose to engage. Everyone is capable, but not all act upon the impulses and motivations associated with dark psychology. Please refer to Chapter 1 for a much more comprehensive look into what makes dark psychology such a unique and fascinating subject area.

**Dark sense of humor psychology:** This area of psychology suggests that those who enjoy a darker sense of humor have higher levels of intelligence. These levels are higher both cognitively and verbally. It shows an ability to analyze and find the wit within "gallows humor." Those who enjoy dark humor also tend to have an ability to practice more readily and to strike the difficult balance of intellectual enjoyment and dark content. It is not necessarily a major component of dark psychology, but it is a related field and could still be another indicator that someone is more likely to practice tactics of dark psychology.

**Dark Singularity:** Dark Singularity is the deepest, darkest, most abhorrent portion of the Dark Continuum. Dark Singularity could be thought of as evil. However, it is not simply evil, but what you may call the pinnacle of evil, incomprehensible, and completely outside of the boundaries of normal, predictable, justifiable, rational, and moral human behavior. This area of dark psychology is one few will ever approach, and those who do will be regarded as almost subhuman because of their ability to behave in such unfathomable ways. It is not likely that anyone would ever reach the point of Dark Singularity because it would make the perpetrator almost inhuman in the eyes of others.

**Dark Triad:** This is a term for the three personality types most often associated with the use of dark psychology. Those three personality types are narcissists, Machiavellians, and psychopaths. There is some debate that there is a fourth personality type, the everyday sadist, but the scholarship most frequently focuses on the three personality types listed above. Please note that the term psychopath in this text does not refer to a psychological diagnosis of psychopathy by a medical professional but instead refers to characteristics exhibited as an aspect of someone's personality. For more details about the three personality types of the Dark Triad, read the definitions in this list or return to Chapter Two for an in-depth look at each of them and related personality characteristics.

**Darkness Manipulation:** This term is used to describe the power someone possesses if they are a practitioner of dark psychology. This power can be cultivated if someone chooses to actively pursue and study dark psychology to become a master manipulator and mind controller. However, there is a suggestion from other theories, like the Dark Triad, that certain personality types are more likely to already have the skill of darkness manipulation. It is possibly the result of their dark psychology being closer to the surface of their consciousness than that of most other people.

**Egoism:** This is an obsessive personality trait in which an individual is concerned only with what will benefit them. They are so preoccupied with this goal that they will completely ignore how it may impact those around them. The person's sense of self-importance is so strong that they cannot comprehend why they would need to think about how pursuing their own success may negatively affect others.

**Fatigue inducement:** Fatigue inducement is sleep-deprivation or fatigue-producing acts. Once fatigue is induced, the victim will be so deep into their fatigue that they will begin to change what they are saying and doing so that it will make the perpetrator happy, even if that means lying. This is a common practice within law enforcement and military tactics. The victim is much more willing to be compliant when they have been systematically deprived of rest. This is frequently combined with starvation to create an even stronger effect.

**Gift giving:** Gift giving is what it sounds like, but it is more specific than just giving a present to someone. Gift giving is providing a present or desirable item to someone so that the other person will feel the need to reciprocate. It essentially guilts them into returning the favor in some way, whatever that may be. In other words, this scenario means there are always strings attached to the gift, and the receiver will be reminded about the gift as a way to control and manipulate them into doing something or giving something in return.

**Guilt inducement:** Guilt inducement is the act of making a victim feel guilty by expressing some kind of sadness, or other negative feeling, that can only be alleviated by the victim. This usually comes in the form of a passive-aggressive comment or a comment that is meant to sound caring or thoughtful but instead makes the victim feel they have done something wrong and must do whatever it takes to fix the perceived problem. The victim is under the delusion that they have become the source of the perpetrator's angst and must make amends in whatever way the perpetrator may want.

**Internet predator:** An internet predator may not seem at first to be always closely linked with dark psychology, but when you stop to think about it, the goal of those who engage in cyberbullying, cyberstalking, and other web crimes are predators seeking a victim. That is the core of dark psychology, so dark psychology internet threats are as relevant as face-to-face threats. They still carry with them an intent to create harm that has no evolutionary purpose. The only shared goal in every dark psychology tactic is to control or manipulate. That is also the goal of internet predators. These connections are explored more fully in Chapter 6.

**Light Triad:** The Light Triad is meant to be the direct opposite of the Dark Triad. In this triad, the characteristics are all about performing acts that benefit others rather than victimize others. The three components of the Light Triad are Kantianism, faith in humanity, and humanism. This would be an excellent source of research for those who are studying this text as a way to understand what not to do when interacting with others and how to avoid being associated with negative motives and predatory behavior.

**Love denial:** Love denial is the conscious and purposeful withholding of "love." This can come in the form of refusing to outwardly show affection. It can also come in the form of ignoring the victim until the predator gets what they want. It is meant to push the victim into doing as the predator wants so that the predator will once again "love" the victim and show attention and affection. The use of the word "love" is quite misleading because this act is the antithesis of true love. The perpetrator only does enough to keep the victim as their prey. They are not interested in truly loving the victim.

**Love flooding:** Love flooding is almost self-explanatory because the name says it all. It is the conscious act of completely overwhelming someone with "love." This can come in the form of compliments or affection and is almost always followed by requests for something from the victim. It lures the victim into believing that the predator loves them and that the victim must do what they are being asked to prove they return the love. This goes beyond the common practice of a child saying to a parent, "Mommy/Daddy, I love you so much," and then asking for a toy or candy. Love flooding is much more conscious, less obvious, and the requests are not as benign in nature.

**Machiavellian:** A Machiavellian is someone who uses lies to manipulate others to help them achieve a self-serving goal. What sets apart Machiavellians is their unparalleled ability to verbally and emotionally control others. Their lies are often the product of careful study and preparation so that the victim is completely unaware that they are being coerced into a series of actions already pre-planned by the Machiavellian. They are ruthless and driven only by the need to benefit themselves. What makes them so sinister is the precision with which they craft their lies. It makes them difficult to perceive, even if you're looking for their traits.

**Mind games:** Mind games are not only for the movies. They are actual strategic decisions made to coerce a victim into a sense of powerlessness and to make the perpetrator appear infinitely superior. It is the use of a number of psychological strategies all at once that methodically direct the thoughts, emotions, and actions of the intended victim. Those who use mind games are not only practitioners of dark psychology, at least not laymen. These sorts of tactics may be employed in any number of professions as a way to monitor certain individuals, such as criminals, suspected criminals, captives, or even employees. This is a difficult tactic to master but is also dangerous because it can be so complicated and nuanced.

**Moral disengagement:** When someone is morally disengaged, they have made a conscious choice to "turn off" their moral value in order to commit an immoral act without guilt. They are able to compartmentalize their own conscience in such a way that they will be capable of feeling guilt one moment and completely remorseless the next. This allows them to set aside their humanity when perpetrating some type of victimization or criminal, violent, or deviant act.

**Narcissist:** A narcissist is someone who is completely self-centered and will use lies to manipulate others into believing their grandiose self-concept. They frequently lie to make themselves appear more important. They constantly crave attention. For this reason, they will enjoy being on stage for a large audience. Whatever action they take, it is to serve one purpose, and that is to increase their perceived importance.

**Necrophilia:** Necrophilia is the desire to engage in sexual behavior with a corpse. This may sound difficult to connect to dark psychology because the victim is no longer living. However, there can be a deep-seated connection between dark psychology and necrophilia for a fair number of reasons. First and foremost, necrophilia has been connected to difficulties with achieving intimacy and a need to be in control of the intimate act of intercourse. The necrophile has a much higher sense of control when their victim is a corpse. Second, although not true of all cases, it is possible that dark psychology is what was used to entice the victim into the necrophile's path. The necrophile could be the one who killed the victim, which is a brutal exercise of control over another person. This all points clearly back to dark psychology.

**Priming:** Priming is a type of manipulation that subconsciously affects your decision-making. Priming can be something as straightforward as a verbal signal to something as subtle as product placement in a TV series. It can often be hard to detect unless you are hyper aware of word choice and its effects on your reactions. For example, I might say, "The location was sweltering, like an instant bath in your own sweat, streams pouring down your blistering skin." Within the next minute or two, you may unconsciously begin to feel hot or uncomfortable, perhaps shifting your weight around like you are trying to air out. It could be perfectly pleasant where you are sitting, but the verbal suggestion could be enough to move you to behave in a certain way.

**Psychological entitlement:** This is a person's belief that their self-worth is so high, they are more deserving than others. They do not simply want what is being asked for but truly believe it should naturally be given to them because of their inherent merit. This means they will not be able to understand when they are denied something, no matter how convincing the counter argument may be.

**Psychopath:** A psychopath is someone who acts on impulse and has an absence of empathy. They are often considered highly chaotic because it is unclear when and why they will engage in all manner of manipulative, controlling, and even violent behaviors. What characterizes them to the most is an inability to understand and perceive the emotions of others and how their own actions affect others. They may even enjoy witnessing pain or fear because they cannot understand its negative effect on the victim. They are different from a sociopath because they do not have a merely limited conscience but no conscience at all.

**Reverse psychology:** Reverse psychology has become a common term that most people are familiar with. It is the act of telling someone to do something when, in fact, you want them to do the opposite. This is often effective when the victim is upset with the predator. The predator will say what they want the victim to do, and because the victim is upset and does not want to make the predator happy, they do the opposite. But the predator wanted them to do the opposite all along. These scenarios seem obvious when practiced with small children or in a movie, but reverse psychology is still a common and possibly dangerous tactic within dark psychology.

**Sadism:** Sadism is a desire to inflict pain because of the enjoyment and perhaps pleasure that it brings. A sadist will engage in any number of violent behaviors in order to enjoy some kind of satisfaction from the pain produced. To them, pain and pleasure are synonymous. This could be their own pain or the pain of others.

**Self-interest:** This is similar to the idea of being self-centered but is differentiated by the desire to enjoy material and measurable success for oneself. This often comes in the form of an increased social status or increased financial status. It means that a self-interested person will be motivated by what helps them succeed and will be disinterested in how it may help or harm others.

**Semantic manipulation:** This means the act of using words or phrases with multiple meanings. These word choices allow a predator to deny that they intended a certain interpretation of what they said. This can make the victim feel that they were wrong for thinking the predator meant to hurt them or manipulate them and instead will feel that they were the one who was wrong all along.

**Serial killer:** A serial killer is defined as a killer who commits three or more murders that occur over a length of a month or longer. There is often a gap of time between the murders, which is what differentiates a serial killer from a mass murderer. Serial killers have a deep connection to dark psychology because they often exhibit one, two, or all three personality types within the Dark Triad. Additionally, serial murders often engage in behaviors that manipulate and control their victims, whether that be through tempting them to go with them willingly or torturing them, so the serial killer feels in control of their fear and pain.

**Sociopath:** A sociopath is someone who is clinically diagnosed and who is characterized by antisocial behaviors and a limited conscience. They may understand that a certain act is considered morally wrong, but they will move forward with committing the act anyway. This is what sets them apart from a psychopath, someone with no conscience. They are similar in that they both lack the ability to empathize with others.

**Spitefulness:** Spitefulness is an extreme and consuming need for revenge. Someone who is possessed by spitefulness will have such a powerful urge to retaliate that they will do whatever it takes. They will even risk harm to themselves, as long as it increases the likelihood that they will feel avenged.

**Subliminal influence:** Subliminal influence is the use of embedded visual and auditory stimuli to get the viewer to act in certain ways. This is actually an integral tactic for magicians. They prime you to choose a certain way or use a certain word by using subliminal influencers. This is a highly strategic practice and one that is most common in fields like advertising.

**Withdrawal:** Withdrawal is the act of the predator ignoring the victim in some way. This could mean the predator remains near the victim but will give them the silent treatment. This could also mean the predator completely withdraws from the presence of the victim, leaving the victim alone. This act of depriving the victim of the predator is meant to make the victim actively crave the predator's presence and acquiesce to whatever the predator is demanding of the victim.

# CHAPTER 4
## *Typical Tactics Of Dark Psychology*

You now understand what dark psychology is, its key characteristics, and its key terms. However, part of what makes dark psychology a source of fascination is its tactics. These strategies are what make the perpetrator the puppeteer and the victim an often-unwitting puppet. The purpose of sharing these tactics is not for you to utilize them so much as it is for you to recognize them and avoid them. To that end, each tactic will be explained and then followed by a few ideas on how to detect that tactic and address so you will not be the victim for long, if at all.

## Strategies in Detail

The first strategy we will explore is one of the most basic, and that is deception. Or, more simply put, lying. It seems simple enough at first. You "stretch" or "bend" the truth to make something easier for yourself, and the victim is most likely completely unaware and unharmed. This could be something rather benign, like telling a friend you're running late because of traffic, when in fact you overslept. It's something nearly everyone has done. It is a "small" lie that still benefits the liar. However, within dark psychology, deception is an art form. It is the basis of so many of the atrocities perpetrators commit.

Lying within dark psychology can come in two forms. One would be lying because of careful study and planning. The other is the result of total impulse. Both can be incredibly damaging for a victim, and both have their pros and cons. Planning, of course, has the added benefit that the perpetrator can think through any number of scenarios that may expose their lie. In this way, they can prepare for eventualities and have perhaps another lie ready to back up the first if necessary. The detriment to this kind of lying is that strategic liars almost always have to layer their lies to continue to make them believable over extended periods of time. This means keeping track of who was lied to and what lies they were told. A quick slip could mean the whole set of lies comes tumbling down and exposes the perpetrator. There is also a possibility that the perpetrator will spend so long planning the lie that one of the factors involved will change and ruin the plan, sending the perpetrator back to stage one of their planning. Those perpetrators who lie more impulsively are often good at improvising. They can lie quickly and make it believable, and they can craft it instantaneously. This avoids the tedium of planning and can give the lie less of a "studied" air. This type of lying could also be much easier for someone who plans to do something to the victim shortly after lying that will distract them from the lie. This kind of lying is dangerous because there is a chance that the victim will discover the lie as quickly as it was told. After all, the liar did not take any disruptions or other eventualities into account. Regardless of which kind of lie someone may choose, lying is a cornerstone of dark psychology.

Most of the tips for avoiding a liar or spotting a lie may seem obvious, but it is important to remember that someone well-versed in dark psychology will be lying on a different level than you are used to. The easiest way to investigate whether you are being lied to is to seek concrete evidence of the lie. This may sound devious in itself, but that is only true if you are investigating without just cause. Concrete evidence means something verifiable and tangible, such as a written document or a security video. Be wary of eye-witness accounts. It is entirely possible that you are talking to someone who is also part of the lie or to another victim who will corroborate the lie because they are in the perpetrator's power. An even more simple tactic is to directly confront the individual about the situation and demand they provide the concrete evidence themselves. After all, if they have nothing to hide, there should be no reason that they would withhold that evidence.

The second strategy is cheating. You may be saying to yourself that this one is too obvious. However, a good cheater can make it far fast if they are methodical and careful. Cheating is not just looking at a neighbor's paper during a test. Cheating can also be cheating within a relationship. This kind of cheating is also closely connected to the first strategy, lying. You cannot achieve a successful cheat without the ability to lie. This then ties into a third strategy, denial. A liar who has decided to cheat may indeed get caught. After the perpetrator is caught, their instinct will be to deny the charges. This is not only natural but intentional for someone who uses dark psychology regularly. They may not have expected it, but they will formulate a denial quickly. The denial deflects from the lie and causes you, the victim, to defend yourself instead of the perpetrator defending themselves.

Cheating and denial are closely related, so we will talk about avoidance tactics for both at the same time. A clear sign of cheating is when something appears to come too easily for the perpetrator and is not in line with their normal behavior and/or achievement levels. If it seems abnormal, it more than likely is. Do not be afraid to trust your gut, and again, look for the concrete evidence. To avoid the problems of denial, stick to facts. Present what you know in clear terms that leave no room for denial. After each fact, demand that the perpetrator verifies what you have said so that they cannot try to backtrack later. If they continue to try to deny, then follow your facts with requests for concrete evidence. There is no room for denial when you are asking them to show their innocence. Again, if they are truly innocent, there will be no need to hide anything that proves it.

A perhaps unsuspected dark psychology tactic is apologizing. This is a powerful tool because it is something that has always been presented as positive. After all, we all learned in school that when you cause harm or make a mistake, you must apologize before healing can begin, and then everyone can move forward. A perpetrator is aware of this process and will use apologies to get to you to move on quickly from what went wrong. The danger in this is that you will too easily forget how many times they have committed the offense or may miss a pattern of behavior that would lead you to discover their lies sooner. Apologies also make a victim feel better and more at ease. It seems unlikely that someone who is "evil" would be willing to apologize. We frequently equate apologies to goodness. Just because they said "sorry" does not mean it is true or that they will not engage in the manipulative behavior again.

To avoid the danger of apologies, try to give yourself reflection time after the fact. At that moment, you will be caught up in your emotions, emotions the perpetrator may have stirred up on purpose. After the conversation is over, think through what began the issue. Ask yourself if it was something that could truly be fixed by an apology. Ask yourself if it's something they've done before. Ask yourself if you can think of other times they've used an apology to avoid an uncomfortable situation. Were any of those issues truly resolved? Or did the negative behavior resurface anyway? A good way to make sure an apology is not devoid of merit is to demand that concrete and measurable actions be connected to the apology. If they are sorry, they should also demonstrate altered behavior or present a plan for how they will improve in the future.

Another tactic that may quickly follow an apology is doing favors for you. This may sound kind or even thoughtful, and for a normal person, it may be. But for someone who is using dark psychology to victimize you, the favors serve one purpose, distraction. You will be so caught up in the emotional euphoria that comes from having something done for you that you will neglect to properly assess whether the predator fixed the problem they caused in the first place.

A quick way to spot genuine favors is if the person mentions why they are doing the favor. They may say something like, "I am doing this to show you..." and fill in that blank with whatever issues it is they need to work on. You will know it's meant to be a distraction if it has no discernible connection to what went wrong. It seems to be completely random and unmotivated. This may sound like a positive experience, unexpected kindness, but you must ask yourself if it was something the perpetrator could have easily done on impulse or something that required planning. Ask yourself if it looks like a random act but obviously took some planning. Then ask yourself if it happened right after a problem arose. If that is the case, then they may be trying to make you believe in them again without wanting you to make the connection between the favor and the victimizing act.

Another manipulative strategy is showing sympathy. Again, this may sound ridiculous because showing sympathy is supposed to be a good thing. Showing sympathy is an important way to show that you care about someone else's feelings. You are correct in most cases, but in the case of dark psychology, you may need to think again. The sympathy is only necessary because of what the perpetrator did. They are trying to comfort you when you would not be suffering if they had not victimized you first. As with favors, sympathy is meant to be a distraction from what created the need for sympathy. You will be feeling comforted and cared for, which is a pleasant experience. However, once you take a step back, you will be able to remind yourself that you only need comfort because the perpetrator caused you pain.

If you want to stop negative sympathy, the easiest step is to separate yourself from the perpetrator. You will not be able to reflect and think clearly when the perpetrator can still easily manipulate you with another round of lies, denials, apologies, favors, and more sympathy. They have an arsenal of tactics now to get you to move on from noticing the heart of what they did and why they did it. Another good idea is to present the scenario to someone else you find trustworthy. See what their initial reaction is. As the victim, you may be too close to the situation to see it clearly. An outside perspective may show you just how ridiculous the perpetrator is and how manipulative their behavior is becoming. Even better, ask yourself if there is someone who has been in your place before. Maybe the perpetrator has another victim you could contact who could validate your experiences and help you see your way out of their lies even faster.

Although seeking out other victims could be helpful when they are accessible, if they are inaccessible, the perpetrator may use them to make you feel inferior. They may start comparing you to the other victim or simply another person. This comparison is meant to manipulate you into going on the defensive. Once you do that, you have taken the focus off of the perpetrator and put it on yourself instead. The person they choose to compare you to is also important to notice. They may strategically choose someone who makes you feel inferior in some way or someone you dislike. Either one will create a powerful emotional reaction within you. Now the person you are thinking of is the one they are comparing you to. You have lost sight of the perpetrator again, which is exactly what they want.

When a perpetrator begins to compare you to someone else, it is best to stop yourself before you respond. Ask the perpetrator to give you some time, which they will not like and may throw them off. Then you can assess why they chose that person for comparison. You can also assess if there is a genuine connection between the person they compared you to and the situation at hand. If there is a connection, then they may genuinely be trying to show you how you may be a part of the problem, too. If there is no connection, then the perpetrator's goal was to make you defend yourself and once again distract you from what they did.

If all their other tactics have failed, a perpetrator may try to turn the whole situation on its head by complaining about you. Once again, the focus will be shifted, and you will be on the defensive. They may even try to make it seem like you are the perpetrator, placing themselves in the role of victim. This will most likely cause you to become angry and will almost always cause you to start defending yourself. Defending yourself means they have control again. They are making you do all of the work while they keep pushing your emotional and psychological buttons, creating whatever reaction they want.

When a perpetrator of dark psychology begins to start complaining about you rather than allowing you to confront them, it is best to make yourself and them go back to the beginning. Ask yourself and them what started this conversation or situation in the first place. What was the catalyst for all this chaos? If the answer is the perpetrator, then you have successfully controlled them rather than allowing them to control you. If they continue to try this tactic and complain about you more, then try to pacify them with a compromise. It will lure them into a false sense of security. You could say that you will happily let them confront you about their complaints but only after you have finished having your say. The important part is that you maintain control of the focus of the situation.

If a perpetrator successfully complains about you and has put you on the defensive, it is likely that they will next attempt to lure you into feelings of guilt and shame. For example, if they denied that they lied and used another lie to prove themselves innocent, they may say to you, "It's easy to see you don't trust me. You can't understand how much that hurts me." So now they have successfully complained that you do not trust them and have preyed on your feelings by making you feel bad that you hurt them. This will make your emotional focus shift from righteous anger to guilt and shame. Now you will feel that you are paranoid and cruel to not trust the perpetrator. Even worse, you will be worrying about their feelings when the true victim in all of this has always been you.

This is one of the more difficult tactics to fight against because we have been so programmed to let guilt and shame overtake our emotions. What you could do is let the situation play out and let the perpetrator feel they won. Then later, after you have overcome those feelings of guilt and shame, you can readily walk yourself back through the conversation and assess if you truly did anything wrong in the situation. If the answer is no, then do not let the perpetrator feel in control for long. Force them back into the conversation and start it with the correct focus, which is what the perpetrator did to victimize you.

If a perpetrator is intent on their goal of victimizing you no matter what, they may resort to emotional blackmail. Emotional blackmail is a form of manipulation that uses emotions to get you to act as the perpetrator desires. Since it relies on manipulation, that means it falls into the category of dark psychology. This process has a few steps before the perpetrator will be successful. They will begin by presenting their demand, what they want you to do. It is likely you will resist, whether directly or indirectly. Resistance is a natural part of the emotional blackmailing process. To fight back, the perpetrator will apply more pressure to their demand, perhaps by telling you to do it out of love or that you owe them (perhaps because of one of the favors they performed) or trying to show you why the demand is a good thing. If the pressure does not create the desired effect, the perpetrator will move onto threats. These threats will be related to some of the key terms explored in Chapter 3, like withdrawal and love denial. As with everything a perpetrator does, these threats will be designed specifically to manipulate you and ensure you will remain their victim. It is most likely at this point that you will give up because the threat is too great. This lets the perpetrator not only know that they were successful but also that this is a strategy they can use successfully on you again.

This is perhaps one of the most difficult tactics from which to break free. After all, the threat that they use is tailored to what will provoke the deepest response from you. That is why dark psychology perpetrators are so dangerous. It is more than likely that you will not be able to avoid the emotional blackmail within the context of the moment, and that does not mean you are a failure. What it means is that you are human and susceptible, as we all are, especially when someone is as adept as the perpetrator at manipulation and coercion. What you have to do is assess, when it is all done, whether you have just done something that you would never have considered doing for another person. Imagine the scenario you were just in with another person in your life. If it seems far-fetched or sounds ridiculous, that is because it is. You were victimized. Once you have seen this, the next step is much harder. That is to use a dark psychology tactic to protect yourself and withdraw. If the perpetrator was able to get what they wanted, they are almost guaranteed to do it again and only increase the level of threat the more you resist. To break the cycle, you have to remove yourself entirely. After all, they knew you well enough to manipulate you into behaving in ways you may never have considered before or even find disgusting after the fact. If they have that kind of power already with just a few sentences, imagine how much worse they could become. If you feel tempted to return, find an accountability buddy who keeps you on track. Ask them what they would do and why before you take any action yourself. Surround yourself with allies who are as disconnected from the perpetrator as possible, so they do not also try to victimize them.

The final tactic we will discuss is avoidance. The perpetrator may have exhausted all of their dark psychology resources, but you may be shocked by how effective avoidance can be. As we learned with the Dark Triad, practitioners of dark psychology can often have huge, charismatic personalities that they have designed to lure people in. That is a magnet for victims that can be difficult to resist. After all, if you have been their victim, then there is some part of yourself you entrusted to them. That creates a bond between you, however sinister it may be. Think of it like you are an addict in recovery who quits cold turkey but knows their substance of choice is nearby but not accessible. That is plain torture. It can be the same for a victim. The perpetrator had an undeniable draw for the victim, and giving up on the perpetrator, at least the idea of who the perpetrator is, is like giving up something that made you feel like you never have before.

You have to treat avoidance the same way an addict would maintain their sobriety, and that is through concrete steps, accountability, and a strong support system. The concrete steps could be a combination of the practices mentioned above to avoid being manipulated. Accountability could come in the form of writing reflections when you feel the urge to reach out to the perpetrator. It could be having someone specific you call when you are tempted to find the perpetrator. The strong support system can often be the most difficult component because there is a strong likelihood that the perpetrator will have isolated you from whatever support system you had before you met them. They will also have deluded you into believing those people would never help you again. As with much of what perpetrators say, that is likely a lie. Reach out to those people and reconstruct that support system. They will be what keeps the perpetrator at bay and ensures you will never be victimized again.

This chapter may have you questioning everything about your relationships with others, but that is not its purpose. Be wary of thinking this level of predator is present everywhere. It's not that they don't exist but that few perpetrators are truly successful in deluding victims for long. Only those who lie further along the Dark Continuum will engage nearly every tactic mentioned above in such a way that they can convince a victim to do whatever they want. There are also many perpetrators within dark psychology who will not use many of these tactics because they are more interested in short-term victims than long-term victims. The point is to be aware but not paranoid. Darkness exists, yes, but it is not the dominant trait in humanity.

# CHAPTER 5
*Average People Engaging In Dark Psychology*

You now have a strong foundation in dark psychology concepts and in the most common personality types and tactics used in dark psychology. You may be thinking that you could stop there, but then you would miss out on a fascinating area of dark psychology. Dark psychology is not only used by master manipulators in grand schemes but is also a common tool used by common people. In fact, you most likely have interacted with one of these people within the past year, month, week, or even day and thought they were average or normal. They are not on the darkest end of the Dark Continuum but rather use dark psychology as a part of their everyday lives to drive others to behave in predictable ways. Some may even argue that these kinds of people should not be thrown in with the term dark psychology, but they would be wrong. Always remember that the only key ingredient for dark psychology is a perpetrator who is looking to victimize. That perpetrator may not be seeking to actively harm the other person. What they are doing may not look "harmful" at all. However, that does not change the fact that their actions are construed to manipulate others, often for personal gain, thereby creating the necessary perpetrator/victim dynamic. Dive into this chapter to understand how dark psychology is at work all around you, even if it may look completely innocuous.

## Everyday Manipulators

Dark psychology is most closely associated with manipulation, read as mind-control. Many will resist the label of mind-control, but it cannot be denied that those who practice dark psychology tactics are able to follow a devious formula that provokes others to behave as the perpetrator wants. That is mind-control, but it may be more comfortable for some to label it as manipulation.

Manipulation comes in many forms, as mentioned in the previous chapter, where tactics were explored. What comes next is how those tactics do not exist in silos but rather mix and match to create common personality types that often fall into predictable categories. Some of these may seem obvious, while others may make you defensive, especially if you fall into one of these categories. The goal is not to vilify any of these people but rather to help you recognize that they may be manipulating you, whether to create positive or negative results, or to help you self-assess if you find you fit one or more of these categories. The term manipulator often has a negative connotation. When you hear "manipulator," you think, "bad person." But dare to open your mind just a bit and see how manipulation is not always intended for harm but can instead be a nudge that helps someone improve their life or choices or relationships. Bear that in mind as you keep reading.

## Selfish People

Selfish people sound almost too common to include as part of this grouping, but it is truly connected to dark psychology. All you have to do is imagine someone you would describe as selfish who is or has been close to you personally. Now ask yourself what motivated their decision-making. The answer is obvious: their own benefit. This falls squarely into the Dark Triad under narcissism. Of course, a selfish person is not likely to warrant the label of narcissism, but they may have some traits in common. Recall that person again and ask yourself this time what they would do to get what they wanted. If you are able to list anything that involves lying, even white lies, then you can determine that they manipulated others to get what they want. If you can list any action that was done to make others feel bad or to take action for the person, then once again you can determine that they emotionally manipulated others to get what they want. This again connects to the Dark Triad under the label of Machiavellianism. A selfish person is often willing to "bend the truth" if it will benefit them. They will also engage in behaviors that get them attention or other desirable outcomes.

If you're struggling to think of an example for yourself, then use the example of a child who is spoiled. You could certainly say they were groomed to be selfish, but that does not change that some of the behaviors they engage in can be associated with dark psychology tactics. This can include the classic plot of crying to manipulate a parent's feelings. If the child gets what they want when they cry, they will continue to employ this tactic the next time they don't get their way. They may also use the tactic of love flooding by telling the parent they want to manipulate how much they love them and how important they are and how special. This is often followed by requests for something they want, and if they get it, they will have learned that this is another successful tactic to manipulate those around them.

This simplistic example is not all-inclusive, nor does it seek to vilify spoiled children. What it illustrates is how selfishness is connected to dark psychology, and subsequently dark psychology tactics.

## Leaders

You may have done a double-take when reading this particular subtitle because, unlike manipulator, "leader" often has a strong positive association. After all, leaders are supposed to be those who guide us to greatness and make true and lasting change in the world. None of that is changed by what you will read next, but do not let your definition of leader prevent you from seeing how leaders use dark psychology.

A leader is often charismatic and engaging, so much so that they can convince others to do things they never thought possible. This all sounds great, but when you break it down, you can see the latent dark psychology at work. The first important part of that statement is the personality description. Charismatic and engaging are also descriptors associated with the Dark Triad personality types of a narcissist and Machiavellian. There is an undeniable magnetism in leaders, which is how they become leaders in the first place. The second important item in the initial statement is the word "convince." If someone has to convince you, that means they have to change your mind through what they say and do. In other words, mind-control. They make statements that get you to cry or laugh or nod in agreement. They act in ways that spur you to take action and work later or take on more responsibility because you want to please them or support them. The final important part of the first sentence is, "do things they never thought possible." That could be a source of inspiration from a leader. It could make you stop and think, "Wow, I never thought I could do that." However, that can also be a scary statement to make. You are admitting that another person was able to get you to do something you have never done before or may never have considered doing before. They got you to act out of character. That is a form of mind-control, manipulation, or inspiration. No matter which label you pick, there is still dark psychology at the root of it.

You may be left defeated by this section because you now feel you have failed by following strong leaders or even by becoming one. That is not true. What is true is that leadership can start with the best of intentions, an example of dark psychology being used for positive outcomes, but it may end with that same leader employing those successful tactics for outcomes that only suit their personal motivations. That is the lesson of this section. Do not dismiss all leaders as monsters but rather stop and analyze their statements, actions, tactics, allegiances, etc. before you commit to following them wholeheartedly. Be sure they have earned that trust.

## Salespeople

You have likely already made the connection between sales and dark psychology, especially because it has already been mentioned in this book. Sales are driven by many factors, but the tactics used by salespeople are almost universally associated with dark psychology tactics.

It would be useless to list every single sales tactic, so, instead, we will explore one to help you build the connections on your own and then apply them to other scenarios as needed. The scenario we will look at is celebrity endorsement, an idea that has connections to John Broadus Watson.

The premise is obvious. First, you pick a celebrity. Next, you pick a product. Then you have that celebrity use the product, hold the product, and/or talk about the product in a positive way. While this may seem so obvious that you would never fall for such a dupe, stop and examine your own purchases. If you can name at least one product in your house that you automatically associate with a celebrity, then celebrity endorsement did its job. You do not even have to like the celebrity necessarily. What motivates you to buy the product is something else entirely.

Celebrity endorsements are so effective because they prey upon emotions. Emotional manipulation is more difficult to trace, and that is why it is one of the most utilized tactics in dark psychology. Many people would rather follow their "instincts" than to follow a straightforward and logical path. Ultimately, most people trust themselves above all others. With a celebrity endorsement, salespeople are drawing a connection between a product and a successful person. Now when you see that product, you think of the celebrity. When you think of "celebrity," you think of success. When you think of success, you think of how you want it. You may look back at the product and think of how you are smart enough to be as successful as that celebrity, and maybe, just maybe, if you use that same product, you will get to success sooner. Maybe you think it will make you look like that celebrity or act like that celebrity. This feeds into your fantasies about being someone more than who you are. Who wouldn't want to feel as skilled/beautiful/smart as someone others admire? Society's fascination with celebrity makes this an easy win for salespeople looking for a quick way to catch your attention and teach you to associate them and their product with someone the world has put on a pedestal.

This is only one of many examples of how salespeople use manipulative tactics to make sales. To find out if you are falling prey to your emotions rather than following reason and logic, take a step back. Why do you want the product? What immediate positive effect will it have on your life? Is it truly useful, or does it serve as more of a status symbol? Impulse buying is real, so do not get drawn into a purchase because you are unable to see the dark psychology at work.

### Lawyers

Lawyers can do immense good, but they can also do immense harm. The ways in which they accomplish both are nearly identical, and they often find their source in dark psychology.

Whether you have been directly involved in a criminal proceeding or not, it is not difficult to see the ways in which dark psychology can keep justice from being blind. That is because lawyers are speaking to humans, and humans are fallible beings. Humans are also the only living things who have dark psychology hardwired into them. It is no surprise that a lawyer would use this innate ability to their advantage in court.

As with our other subtopics, imagine a scenario. A trial is being held for murder. The evidence is presented, the jury reaches a verdict, and the defendant is declared guilty. The prosecutor has successfully won the case. Then a technicality allows the defense to call for a mistrial. Everything starts over. The same evidence is presented, the jury reaches a verdict, but this time the defendant is declared not guilty. This seems ludicrous. After all, if the evidence did not change, the verdict should remain stable. The answer should be clear. However, it still happened, so the next step is to determine how and why.

The how is not difficult to pinpoint. The defense lawyer most likely used dark psychology tactics to come at the jury in new and more convincing ways. After all, they had the first trial to see what worked and what did not. Now, they have a new opportunity to try a different angle. Again, the evidence did not change. The lawyer simply presented it in a new way. This could be as simple as adjusting their tone or changing their phrasing. However, these subtle changes can reap massive results if the jury is susceptible to these dark psychology tactics. The lawyer only needs to produce reasonable doubt, so if they can flip their words around in such a way that they plant the seed of doubt in the jury, then that seed is left to grow into a not guilty verdict.

What you need to recognize in this scenario is the why. Why did the verdict change? It changed because one lawyer more successfully manipulated the jury than the other. The jury, for whatever reason, felt the need to side with the defense. Notice the word "felt" in that sentence. It is very intentional because it points to how emotions cannot be entirely removed from human decisions, even in something as high stakes as a murder trial. Impartial is practically impossible. Everyone will come with a bias, so all the lawyer has to do is successfully manipulate those biases to be amplified or muted when someone makes their decision. This is also why the most successful lawyers are not known for how they find key evidence or present a logical case. Those may be factors in their success, but they are more often known for being able to play to the jury, question witnesses, or present powerful opening and closing statements. Their ability to play with words, and therefore play with emotions, is what makes them good, and it is also what makes them practitioners of dark psychology.

**Politicians**

This section may have some nodding their heads in agreement or others cringing and thinking about skipping this section. You should continue anyway because this is an all-encompassing discussion of politicians, not one which takes a particular side.

First, stop and think about the definition of a politician. They are intended to be a public servant, someone who serves the interests of the people, their constituents. Next, think about what a politician does. They make decisions that impact others, including themselves, and argue how those decisions are in the best interest of their constituents. So far, this may sound like a lesson on government, but stop and break down the who and the what behind a politician.

A politician is a person, perhaps a person you could say is just like any other. This could be true, but what you may be leaving out of your assessment is the plain and simple fact that politicians are public figures. Public means they are put on display for all to see. But not at all times. Politicians have carefully planned schedules. They know where they are going, who they will be seeing and talking to, and who will be watching them. That means they are able to curate themselves. The use of the word curate is meant to draw attention to how politicians craft a public persona. They would have you believe that the person you watch on television is the same person you would casually meet on the street. More often than not, that is a lie. After all, think of the countless scandals that have ruined a politician. The public is frequently shocked by such revelations. The politician would not have ruined their career and/or reputation if the public already knew they were the kind of person who engaged in such behavior. You may also be thinking of many politicians who survived after such scandals. They survive such scandals because they were so successful in convincing their constituents with their persona that the public chooses to overlook those misdeeds in favor of the persona they bought into. Therefore, the who behind a politician is often misleading, as it is a carefully manufactured and planned creation, not an actual human being who behaves in those ways at all times.

A politician is engaged in decision-making, and as such, they are privileged with a certain amount of authority and power. Recall the experiment explored earlier in which a group of people entered a fake jailhouse as peers but quickly succumbed to the power of labels. Those who were labeled as an authority began to engage in uncharacteristic and disturbing behaviors. This is not to say that all people in power will be corrupted by that power, but it does mean you should pause and evaluate thoroughly how that power is being wielded. You should also assess if the power is being used consistently. A politician's power means other, less powerful people will be drawn to them. This places them in a prime situation to become victims if the politician chooses to be a perpetrator. A politician's power means others with power, often those with more power, will try to manipulate that politician into using their power for the other's benefit. It quickly becomes a tangled web of complicated motivations and allegiances. What is most notable, however, is that all of these power dynamics are made possible because the person with power allows that label to indeed place them above those who are powerless. After all, there are plenty of politicians whose constituents may voice their opinion to vote to pass a bill or law, but the politician votes against it. When this occurs, then you have to dig deeper into what the politician does versus what they are supposed to do. They are making decisions, but how consistently do those decisions align with the cares and concerns of the people they claim to represent. You may or may not be surprised to find that nearly every single one has voted contrary to their constituents' demands at least once. That is because they are human, and they are often engaging in the use of dark psychology.

It is easy to see now how a politician is set up to be a devotee to dark psychology. Their persona is in line with both characteristics of a narcissist and a Machiavellian. Their motivations, whether personal or political, can also be tied to Machiavellianism or psychopathy. You could even argue that politicians, along with most others in positions of extreme power, will almost always fit into one or more of these personality types within the Dark Triad. This is not to say all politicians will engage in such behaviors, but it should make you pause and examine how and why they became a politician in the first place and who benefits from their decisions. It could be a dark journey, but it is much more satisfying to understand how they may be engaging in mind-control practices than to unwittingly fall for their carefully laid traps. Never fear to question. Questioning can lead you to discoveries that keep you safe from the circle of victimization created by the most sinister perpetrators.

## Analyzing Motivation

This chapter shows you the ease with which a common person may, in fact, be using dark psychology for nefarious purposes. You may also be questioning how many of your decisions are truly good versus motivated by the propensity for dark psychology that lies in all of use. Here are a few questions to help you break down yours and others' decisions to discover the true motivation.

1. Why did you initiate this action or interaction?
2. Who does this benefit directly in the short-term and in the long-term?
3. How much, if at all, did you "stretch the truth" in your interaction?
4. Is what you're saying designed to build a stronger relationship with those you are interacting with?
5. Is your approach to the situation based on the desire for mutually positive outcomes?

This is not an exhaustive list, of course, but it is a great way to guide your thought process as you analyze motivations and strategies that may be at play in your life. No one can be expected to avoid dark psychology entirely. As has been stated previously, it is entirely human to have thoughts and take actions that are designed to victimize others. What is being asked of you and of everyone is that actions are not taken without self-reflection. These questions also prompt you to reach a new level of awareness. Note that the word is "awareness," not "paranoia." These questions are not something you should have to visit daily but only when you are in a more dangerous and serious situation. Beyond that, they may be a fun exercise to analyze ways you may have succumbed to a salesperson's tactics, for example, but that is not the goal. The goal is to put the power back in your hands and leave you feeling empowered to understand the dark psychology at play all around you.

# CHAPTER 6
*The Dark Side Of Dark Psychology*

You will encounter dark psychology tactics on a daily basis. That is inevitable. What is far less likely is that you will be pulled to the darkest end of the Dark Continuum. As you may recall from the chapter on dark psychology terms, the Dark Continuum is a spectrum with which to measure how close someone's behavior approaches true evil. This deeply dark end of the spectrum, a place where absolute evil exists, is known as the Dark Singularity. Of course, it is difficult to define what "pure evil" means, but it is not too hard to see how many notorious figures throughout history can fall on the darker end of the Dark Continuum. These are the nightmarish individuals whose motivations often cannot be found and whose actions defy what we understand to be within the scope of human possibility. These are the people you would call inhuman, calculating, ruthless, and chaotic. This chapter is a look into what it means to take dark psychology too far and yet how the darkness of only one perpetrator can still pull in a massive number of victims.

## Breaking Down the Dark Terms

Before you can properly understand the dark psychology behind the darkest of criminals, you have to understand some dark terms that will help guide you. The Dark Continuum is first. This continuum does not have a set beginning but does have a set end. You could think of the beginning as mere thoughts of victimizing someone for no clear evolutionary purpose. It could be a fleeting desire, but it still falls on that spectrum. From an action point of view, you could think of the beginning as the impulse to violently strike out as a gut reaction to someone doing something you do not like. At that moment, all you want to do is kick, hit, punch, but you do not. At this end, you are still in control and are still self-aware enough to stop yourself from engaging in dark behavior. Some of the stops along this continuum would be many of the personality types we have discussed. A selfish person who is relatively harmless would be low on the continuum. A manipulative leader with Machiavellian tendencies would be further along. Anyone who has a personality type that closely aligns with those of the Dark Triad would be even further up. Those who possess elements of all three personality types of the Dark Triad are beginning to approach the end of the continuum.

The end of the Dark Continuum is defined as the Dark Singularity, the pit of inhumane and unfathomable behavior. It may be tempting to place many famous criminals' acts on the end of the Dark Continuum, but that is very difficult, if not impossible, to achieve. That is not to say that those who approach this end are worthy of sympathy or even forgiveness but to illustrate that these individuals often have other contributing factors that have placed them closer to the Dark Singularity.

This leads us to the term Dark Factor. Dark Factor is a measure of how likely someone is to engage in dark behavior and to use dark psychology tactics when interacting with others. Dark Factor is not something you can claim a person has had since birth, but you can make the claim that the Dark Factor is stronger in some individuals than in others. Some of the experiences that could increase someone's Dark Factor include an abusive childhood, neglect, an abusive relationship, a traumatic event, a traumatic injury (often a head injury), and more. Some readers may find themselves bristling at this list because they have experienced some of these traumas or someone they love has and is a completely decent and wonderful human being. That is possible, maybe even more likely. However, that does not negate the fact that these triggers can take someone who was already without a conscience and push them into behaviors that approach the Dark Singularity. Connecting these events to these behaviors is also what can enable us to detect these individuals before they get out of control. It is a matter of seeing the warning signs and using them to understand where a person's behavior may go next.

Once a person's Dark Factor is taken into account, then their level of Darkness Manipulation comes into play. Darkness Manipulation is a person's ability to use dark psychology tactics effectively. Someone may have a large amount of Dark Factor, fall within the Dark Triad, and settle on the dark end of the Dark Continuum but still not be a successful criminal or manipulator. That is because their Darkness Manipulation is not as masterful as others. It is not a matter of knowing the tactics but of knowing how and when to use them. A strategy such as gift giving, or withdrawal, is an effective tactic only if the perpetrator has chosen something that will motivate the victim to behave as desired. If the perpetrator chooses the wrong tactic to victimize, they will fail at their manipulation and get caught. This could mean that their Dark Factor is stunted by the criminal justice system because they were caught early in their darkness development. It could also mean that their failure will teach them, and their Darkness Manipulation will only increase with time. There is no set formula for how this will work out, but it is important to recognize all of these nuances at play and how they tie in together to create a person who may come dangerously close to the Dark Singularity.

### Historical Dark Manipulators

The list of dark manipulators throughout time would be extensive indeed, so this list is meant to be a brief exposure that uses some well-known examples. Well-known examples are still relevant because they will help you take your prior knowledge and combine it with your new knowledge about dark psychology. This will give you a fresh and valuable perspective about how and why certain dark figures were able to come to power and to such devastating effect.

Our first historical figure is **Al Capone**. Not everyone may be interested in Mob related history, but Al Capone is a worthy subject for study because of the traceable dark factors and dark tactics that directly contributed to his criminal life.

The first factor at play is Al Capone's childhood. From a young age, he became involved in gang violence. This is how he suffered a facial injury that resulted in the nickname "Scarface." It is likely that he was drawn into the gangs through the use of rudimentary dark psychology tactics. A gang could offer protection and a sense of belonging. These are tempting enticements for a child who may not have had a sense of safety or belonging before. This is a kind of base-level brainwashing. A younger person is more susceptible, of course, which means they are drawn in and stay in because they've never known anything else. This initiation into crime and criminal thinking is a clear indicator that raises Al Capone's Dark Factor. He was likely taught how to use moral disengagement to compartmentalize his conscience from his actions whenever necessary. Instead of seeing the negative impact of his actions, he saw the benefits it would bring him and the gang who had welcomed him. That would make it much easier to frequently engage in criminal acts without any pangs of remorse. Without those early experiences, it is unclear when or if he would have turned to his life of organized crime.

The next noteworthy strategy in Al Capone's history was his use of Machiavellian tactics to groom politicians and media associates into believing he was a good guy. He created a persona that drew in these people and led them to believe his intentions were ultimately in the best interest of everyone. His lies and charisma drew them in and kept them in line with what would most benefit him and his criminal allies. As he learned from his early experiences, it does not take much to draw someone in if they are craving attention, belonging, or safety. Those motivations would entice dozens of people to also morally disengage and somehow believe that aiding and abetting Al Capone was the right thing to do. That is an obvious portrait of someone using dark psychology on a regular basis and with selfish intentions. This careful manipulation is perhaps part of why gang violence at the time escalated to new heights before anyone attempted to take down Al Capone. Even now, he is a fascinating figure who is the center of many films, books, and TV show adaptations. His charm is still convincing people to almost idolize him. His name is known, for better or for worse, because of the ways in which he used dark psychology to build his criminal empire.

Another notorious individual who plagues the minds of society at large is **Jeffrey Dahmer**. If you are unfamiliar with his crimes, he engaged in kidnapping, torture, rape, mutilation, murder, and cannibalism of young men and boys. His crimes fall on the very dark end of the Dark

Continuum and would rank among those crimes deemed inhuman by many. Although you may feel you can never reach an understanding of why this behavior occurred, you can benefit from understanding how the Dark Factor in Jeffrey Dahmer's life built up over time and led into the explosive and violent behavior he displayed later in life.

As with many serial killers, Jeffrey Dahmer's childhood is a potential and likely source for why his Dark Factor reached such substantial heights and brought him so close to the Dark Singularity. Interviews and books by Dahmer's parents do not point to obvious sources for his eventual deviant behaviors, but it only takes a moment to read between the lines and find them.

First, his parents were not deeply involved in his life from a young age. Their marriage was tenuous, and so they devoted themselves to other things, often leaving Dahmer to himself. This isolation meant he was left unchecked and could develop antisocial behaviors without early or strategic intervention. Since his parents' marriage was unhappy, he frequently witnessed verbal altercations between them, which may have made him wary of romantic relationships and unsure of how to develop positive relationships.

When his parents did get divorced finally, his isolation increased because his mother and brother left, ending contact with him, and his father was disengaged from him. At this time, some deviant behaviors that pointed to psychopathy began to show. He started finding dead animals, collecting their carcasses, and then mutilating them to create startling displays. This kind of cry for help left him to fall deeper and deeper into the psychopathic tendencies he already possessed.

This shows his connection to the Dark Triad, a psychopath who lacks empathy and a conscience. Couple this with his inability to create positive social relationships, and you are left with the undeniable chaos that created his violent and unpredictable behavior. Another indicator of his psychopathy was the fact that he described his desire to kidnap, torture, rape, kill, and cannibalize as a compulsion. Dark psychology lacks an evolutionary motive, and that is certainly true in the case of Jeffrey Dahmer.

The next figure we will analyze is John Wayne Gacy, Jr. He, like Dahmer, was a psychopath who was likely drawn into criminal behavior by a difficult childhood. Of course, not every serial killer has a terrible childhood, and not everyone who has a terrible childhood will become a serial killer. What is relevant is how we can use an understanding of dark psychology and the Dark Factor to see how and why Gacy developed into such a disturbing murderer. For those who may be unfamiliar with his story, he is often referred to as the "Killer Clown" and was responsible for the rape, torture, and murder of a large number of young men and boys over a period of six years and buried them beneath his home.

Gacy's descent on the Dark Continuum can be connected to his father. His father was an alcoholic who also subscribed to the misogynistic view that every young boy should engage exclusively in "manly" pursuits, like sports and hunting and outdoor activities. Instead, Gacy preferred cooking and gardening and other activities that would be deemed too "girly" by his father. Gacy was constantly disappointing his father in this way, and his father made his disappointment clear. This meant Gacy repressed these behaviors and therefore repressed his homosexuality. He buried this part of his identity in an attempt to please his father.

At this point, Gacy may seem like the victim, but what comes next shows a shift from victim to perpetrator. His first victims were his family and community. He was so intent on denying his homosexuality that he first convinced a woman to marry him and start a family with him. He may have been pushed to hate his homosexuality, but he made a conscious choice to find a wife and manufacture a life that would be approved by his father. This was only the beginning of his lies.

After he fixed himself as the devoted husband and father, he slipped and was found guilty of sodomizing a young boy. He was convicted and incarcerated. While incarcerated, his father died, which is perhaps the stimulus that pushed him into a deeper spiral down the Dark Continuum. He felt that perhaps it was his conviction that made his father die of shame and humiliation. Gacy then made it his mission to be an even more convincing "upstanding" figure. He started a business and became a fixture in the community who was well-known and liked. Here is the foundation for his dark psychology. He created a world based entirely on lies. What motivated him was his desire to convince others that he was an entirely different person. This Machiavellian mentality was immensely successful.

This leads us to the most disturbing and sinister part of his development along the Dark Continuum. Gacy created a character called Pogo the Clown. He would dress as a clown and perform at children's parties and other community gatherings. His Darkness Manipulation, especially when performing as Pogo, was absurdly powerful. Parents were willing to entrust their children to him. They would even encourage their children to play with Pogo. Gacy had found the perfect persona that would draw in his prey and their parents alike. It would be incredibly difficult to suspect evil would come from a businessman who is deeply involved in the community and plays a harmless clown. That is exactly what made his Darkness Manipulation so skillful. He had the draw of a narcissist, the lying capabilities of a Machiavellian, and the lack of empathy of a psychopath. His Dark Factor became so rooted in the Dark Triad that it is not difficult to see how he came so close to the Dark Singularity.

An undeniable connection exists between dark psychology and cults. Cult leaders are extremely adept at using dark psychology tactics to attract followers and to keep them committed against their better judgment. That is why we will next look at **Charles Manson**. Charles Manson is known for his "family" of followers and the shocking murders that they committed in the late sixties.

There is no need to dig too deeply into Charles Manson's childhood, although there it does point to how his Dark Factor could have developed from a young age. His mother was a sex worker and alcoholic who eventually abandoned him by the age of twelve. He was left to find his own way, and that may have been a contributing factor in his development as a devious and manipulative individual.

Charles Manson eventually decided that he should form the Manson Family, a group of people who enjoyed the use of LSD and psychedelic mushrooms and who also committed to believing that Manson was a new Messiah who had prophetic visions. You may be shaking your head in disbelief at this point. Who could be so delusional that they would fall for such a scheme? That is where the majority of dark psychology tactics come into play.

The initial tactic used by most cult leaders is charisma and ego, the classic narcissist. The cult leader will appear to be immensely charming and engaging, someone who it feels like can speak to your very soul. The cult leader so strongly believes in themselves that the followers believe it, too. The followers have often never known such confidence, so when someone is so self-assured and enticing, the followers fall in love, not necessarily with the leader, but with the persona they present. It is an intoxicating blend of kindness, charm, and confidence that is hard to resist when your defenses are down.

One of the key tactics utilized by nearly every cult leader is isolation. Cult leaders know that if they separate a person from their support system, the only one they can turn to is the cult leader. It creates a dangerous dependence on the cult leader. Cult leaders also know that it is easier to isolate someone who is in need emotionally. Those who are depressed or anxious or lonely will be drawn in by the opportunity to belong to a community that welcomes them. It is likely that the cult leader will then engage in love flooding and compliments and gift giving as a way to show the person how generous the leader is and how caring. Once the follower is immersed in this codependent relationship, then the cult leader can resort to the crueler tactics, such as threatening withdrawal and love denial. Then the follower will find themselves rejected from the community and with no one to help them because they have isolated themselves so completely from the outside world and outside support. The only choice is the cult leader.

Cult leaders like Manson are also talented at brainwashing. This includes the social-isolation described above as well as fatigue-inducement and starvation. When the followers are not allowed to sleep, and it is the cult leader who is withholding sleep, they will often do whatever is asked of them in order to finally sleep. The same is done with food. In the case of Manson, he also used hallucinatory substances to convince his family that he had prophetic visions. The mental states of his family members were in total disarray, which left them open to complete and total mind-control.

Manson's use of Dark Manipulation was so skilled that he never actually committed a murder. He did not commit the murders, but he was able to convince multiple people to go out multiple times to kill others. This level of mind-control is difficult to understand. Few people believe themselves capable of murder without any clear motivation, but dark psychology made it possible for Manson to control his followers and coerce them into behaving in uncharacteristic and violent ways. His control was so absolute that, even as they faced the death penalty, his followers would sing and giggle and make faces throughout the trial process. Their minds became the playgrounds in which he lived out his grandiose fantasies of power and prestige, a true practitioner of dark psychology.

These historical examples only begin to scrape the surface of the depravity that exists in many criminals. However, it does show that the Dark Continuum is vast. With enough Dark Factor and enough skill with Darkness Manipulation, it is possible to come incredibly close to the Dark Singularity. When you hear about the next notorious criminal who lands in the spotlight, trace back through their personal history and see if you can find the signs and detect where they put dark psychology to work before they were finally stopped.

# CHAPTER 7
## *Dark Psychology And Social Media*

Nearly every modern person of a certain age is guilty of connecting their lives to social media, whether it is through Facebook, Instagram, Twitter, Snapchat, or YouTube. We are constantly plugged into a stream of media that is ever-changing and highly engaging. The world wide web is at the tips of your fingers at nearly every minute of every day. However, there is latent darkness at work behind social media. The internet opened a vast portal into knowledge and connection, but it also created a highly convenient and exploitable method for perpetrators to find and harass more victims. This chapter is meant to dive into how social media can be a hotbed of dark predators whose posts and responses employ a variety of dark psychology tactics that have real-world consequences. After all, what predator would shy away from being a faceless entity in a virtual world? Anonymity is the perfect cloak for someone whose sole purpose is to victimize those around them.

### How Social Media Invites the Darkness

When social media first began, the intent was to allow people to stay in contact, to feel more involved with friends' lives, and to put on display whatever part of our lives we most wanted to show. That initial intent was perhaps good, but the way in which it has evolved has left a huge opening for dark predators.

Social media is susceptible to Dark Manipulators first and foremost because it is so easy to be anonymous. The plethora of various usernames and account profiles are nothing more or less than what the user makes of them. They can be from anywhere, like anything, change age, gender, nationality, and more, all with the click of a few buttons and the typing of a few words. There are hundreds upon hundreds of profiles that are closer to being characters than they are to being human beings. This idea has a profound connection to narcissism and egoism. The difference is the person who is at the center of narcissism or egoism may not be a person at all but is instead a fantasy person created by a perpetrator. This makes them free to be whatever they want, even if the person they create acts in ways they never would in real life.

Social media, in many ways, encourages narcissism because your posts are intended to generate attention for yourself, whether positive or negative. It is difficult to argue that a post can truly be selfless when your name is always attached to what you post. Even reposting someone else's content is, in a way, showing support for whatever that content is. You want anyone who follows you to understand that you like and support that content so much that you want others to see it. The content is irrelevant when you look at social media from this angle. You could try to argue for days that your intent was to start a positive conversation or to make someone smile, but it all ultimately points back to you. You wanted something, some kind of response, and your post gave you what you wanted. That could be satisfaction at spreading an idea you support or the simple joy of having others like what you have to say. The motivation is always tied up in how it reflects back on the user. This is an addicting setup because you can place yourself on stage but let other people technically decide whether they want to pay attention. It makes you feel like you are less of a performer on social media, but the fact is everyone is performing on social media. They are performing whatever version of themselves that they want the world to see, understand, and interact with. That is why so many posts are designed to provoke likes or retweets or even negative responses. The performer ultimately wants to know someone is watching the performance.

Dark Manipulators also flock to social media because it is a platform that allows you to say highly inflammatory things and be admired for it. There are countless posts which many people would never dare say as a statement made to another person, and yet those posts are put up and interacted with again and again. The fact that you do not have to see the person on the other side allows you to more readily use moral disengagement. The profile you are viewing does not feel like a person, so you can justify that it is okay to say something much harsher than you would in person. You morally disengage actual reality from virtual reality and decide that each level of existence has its own unique morality. When you look at it that way, it is obvious how social media invites the influences of dark psychology. It is almost a fantasy world in which you can say whatever you want and show whatever you want and still go out into reality and act in completely different ways. This is also perhaps why many people will spend their time together still glued to a screen. They are no longer interested in interacting in reality as much as they are interested in interacting with their virtual reality. Just as we discussed the way a politician curates their self-image, that is precisely what you do when you create and use a social media profile. This is inherently Machiavellian. You are lying to show only those parts of yourself that will benefit you. Even if you post something unflattering and then talk about working on yourself, you are asking whoever views that post to give you attention, to celebrate you or support you. That makes you feel good, and that is enough of a motivation to call what you are doing Machiavellian and narcissistic. Lying to manipulate and centering yourself is at the heart of social media. That is already two-thirds of the Dark Triad.

Once anonymity and facelessness are established, the next dark temptation is to act on impulse. Social media posts are like a live film, constantly evolving within the moment and completely uncensored. If too much time passes, the momentum is lost, and the post may lose steam. Therefore, social media invites impulsivity and chaos. There is no time for reflection after the initial post. What happens next is in real-time, so you have to post now or miss out. There is an addiction to staying on top of the latest trends or the latest news, so waiting would leave you behind. Since you have to act quickly, you are robbed of the time it would take to think through what you are going to say, how you are going to say it, and whether you should be saying anything at all. Within that moment, you are being invited to take the fleeting thoughts related to dark psychology and perform them live, right now, without thought. Social media almost demands that you post your initial gut reaction, fraught with intense emotion, and full of uncharacteristic vitriol. That is how you bring in the last part of the Dark Triad. A psychopath has no conscience, lacks empathy, and moves with impulsivity. You are not necessarily a psychopathic personality generally, but social media drives you to act in psychopathic ways. You set morality and reason aside to react at that instant rather than miss out on the chance to stay involved in whatever is happening. This causes users to speak and act in ways that are not connected to the reality of who they are. When you respond to a post at that moment, you have not taken the time to think about the other person's reaction beyond the thought that you want them to react. You do not consider their perspective in a humane way but only as a way to gauge how successful you were with your own posting practices. You also cannot engage your conscience if you respond at that precise moment. You are not thinking through whether it is "right" or "wrong" but rather whether it will be well-received or frequently noticed. Attention is attention, whether positive or negative, so you dive into the chaos of impulsive posting. You have behaved as a psychopath may. Now the Dark Triad in social media is complete.

### Dark Social Media Types

The first part of this chapter shows the ways in which the internet, and specifically social media, create a breeding ground for dark psychology and all that it entails. This section is an exploration of some of the types of social media abusers and what each of them does to create victims. It is important to establish that these actions, although done in a virtual setting, have real-life implications. The victim is no less victimized because what they are experiencing is happening online rather than face to face. The perpetrators are also no less dangerous because they are far away and faceless. The danger is real, so read on to learn more about the most common dark social media types.

You may already be familiar with the term **keyboard warrior**, but you may not fully understand what it has to do with dark psychology. First, a keyboard warrior is defined as someone who initiates intense virtual interactions to defend or promote a particular viewpoint. A keyboard warrior has deeply entrenched beliefs that are at the heart of every post and comment they make. This may not sound terrible at first. After all, someone who has strong convictions can often be appealing or admirable. What is dangerous, however, is when the beliefs they subscribe to are harmful are downright misinformed. What is also dangerous is when they believe something positive, but are so determined to beat their opposers down, that they go too far.

Keyboard warriors will most often engage in dark psychology tactics that are verbal since, as the name implies, they are only able to type rather than take physical action. One typical example would be semantic manipulation. A keyboard warrior will word something in such a way that the meaning can be manipulated. This is a trap for whoever responds to the keyboard warrior because then the keyboard warrior can instantly fight back and claim that the responder misunderstood what they were saying. This gives the predator a twofold victory. First, they controlled their victim's response, and second, they undermined their victim's authority by making them sound inept at understanding what the perpetrator has to say. It is a vicious cycle that can go back and forth and even cause the victim/perpetrator dynamic to be flipped if two keyboard warriors decided to engage in the discussion. There can even be collectives of keyboard warriors who work in conjunction with one another, creating a pack-mentality that also encourages uncharacteristic behavior and increases animosity towards others.

Keyboard warriors will also engage in dark psychology tactics that seem positive to other users and make them take the side of the perpetrator. They may try to use love flooding in a virtual way by liking comments that are supportive of them or excessively praising those who reinforce what the keyboard warrior is saying. This makes those responders feel validated and valued, so they are more likely to defend the keyboard warrior even as they devolve into more heated and perhaps aggressive rants. This is almost like the creation of a virtual cult. The leader, the keyboard warrior, has a curated persona that is strong and confident that others flock to. Once that initial charm has drawn someone in, it becomes easier and easier to use moral disengagement to separate the virtual from the real. Then the keyboard warrior has a following, a group of fellow virtual devotees who will rush to defend and aid their leader. Online communities have the same risk factors as those in real life.

Another dark social media type is the **cyberbully**. Bullies have been a constant concern for families and young people for decades. They are self-appointed predators who often victimize others to make themselves feel more important or to distract from their own problems. Before the internet, these bullies were much easier to track because they had to interact with someone in person in order to bully. There was a concrete action or a concrete statement that could be witnessed and documented and punished as needed. The internet, however, has given them a chance to be anonymous and faceless and has extended their victim pool to include anyone, not just those within their immediate social circle or community. It also does not require any level of physical intimidation. A cyberbully intimidates because of what they say much more than what they do. This means they engage in emotional bullying, which is much more damaging psychologically. A bruise can heal, but the comments a cyberbully makes have made an emotional impression on the victim that is not a visible wound.

A cyberbully may sound like something insubstantial, but there is a characteristic of cyberbullying that makes its marks even more lasting. Once something has been posted on social media, it is there for the world to see and often there forever. There are some regulations on social media sites now that allow others to report harmful comments or content, but that does not stop dozens or even hundreds of people from seeing it and perhaps screenshotting it for later. This means that the cyberbully's words do not disappear after they are said but are there to be read and experienced again and again and again. This means the victim cannot walk away from the experience after the cyberbully has made their statement but instead must revisit that feeling every time they see the post or others mention the post. This can keep the victim in a constant cycle of anxiety and self-consciousness that is crippling. That is why cyberbullying is potentially even worse than in-person bullying. The perpetrator is harder to find, and what the perpetrator does is practically immortalized on the internet for years to come. It is also possible for a cyberbully to move their bullying off of mainstream social media and onto alternative platforms that may even encourage and support their behavior. The cyberbully can keep on bullying the victim, perhaps without the victim's knowledge, but the cyberbully can still get a sadistic satisfaction out of watching their victim be victimized again by others on other platforms.

A cyberbully is most likely to fall under the label of narcissist or Machiavellian. They can be narcissists because they are attention-seeking. By making the victim seem lesser, they, in turn, seem more important or better. They also want everything to point back to them, and cyberbullying makes them feel superior because they were able to bring down their victim. They can be considered Machiavellian because they can easily post lies with impunity. There is no fact-check button that can be pressed on social media. The cyberbully has the ability to make up whatever lie they want about the victim. They can also tailor their lies to the victim by first analyzing the victim's profile. Their analysis can help them pinpoint the victim's weaknesses and therefore make their lies more strategic. They will know how to provoke the exact response that suits their needs.

The final dark social media type we will explore is the **cyberstalker**. A cyberstalker is someone who uses the internet to track someone. This is not quite the same as a real-life stalker. A cyberstalker can be almost undetectable if they wish. What they are interested in is following the victim, and if the cyberstalker has created a convincing profile, that is easy to do on social media.

Social media is not entirely about posts. It also includes pictures. This is what a cyberstalker would most want to see. If the victim shares their location or mentions that they always go to a certain place, then the cyberstalker has the knowledge to find you in real life if they want. They can use the backgrounds of your photos to pinpoint what parks you visit, what stores you shop in, what theaters you frequent, what school you or your kids attend. Those photos can tell them immense amounts of information about you and your daily life. For example, many apps can be used to track your exercises, such as a running route. It is likely you or someone you know has posted their run before with the time circled because they achieved a personal record. This has the appearance of being a great celebration for someone's achievement, but to a cyberstalker, it is a literal map of where to find you and possibly even when you run, if that was included in the picture posted.

Cyberstalkers are perhaps the most concerning dark social media type. If they choose to stalk you but do not engage with your social media profiles, you could be stalked and never know it. The only way you may find out is if the cyberstalker decides to bring their stalking practices to reality. They may also be following you in other ways than only on social media. If you have left your accounts vulnerable, they may be tracking your emails or apps and use them to gain sensitive information about your personal life. They will dig into whatever part of your life they can get to if it is available on the internet. They are also menacing because they can always change profiles or names if you do detect them. Be wary of who you accept into your social media circles. If someone has victimized you before, it is likely they will seek to victimize you repeatedly, if they can.

This chapter may sound like a massive, dire warning about the ills of social media, but before you go delete all of your accounts, stop and think. There are responsible ways to use the internet and social media that do not have to stray into the Dark Continuum.

What you need to do is start with yourself. Think about your own profile and what it contains. Ask yourself why you post certain things or why you respond to certain people. What are your motivations? What is your goal? Does your profile truly show who you are as a person? Does what you say virtually match what you say in real life? The goal is to make virtual reality and true reality as close to the same as possible. This can ensure that you are always acting within the boundaries of your moral character and will make you actively engage in the empathetic practices you would use in face-to-face interactions.

The next step is to think before you post. It is so tempting to fall into the instant gratification of typing a response at that exact moment. However, that is exactly how you allow the dark psychology at work within you to become a prominent part of who you are instead of a merely human tendency that you do not indulge. Stop and think about what you will say, how you will say it, and whether you should respond in the first place. Evaluate if you are just making yourself a target for a keyboard warrior and are starting an argument you never wanted to be part of. More often than not, you will find it's not worth it. It is much healthier to walk away. Dark psychology is not all bad, but giving in to your dark tendencies without careful care and consideration can pull you to a place on the Dark Continuum where you never wanted to be.

The final step to ensure you do not fall into the dark traps of social media is to protect your accounts. Make sure you are only inviting people into your social circle that you trust. If you do allow most people to follow you, then be deliberate with what you post and how much you share about your life. Ask yourself if what you are sharing would make a better conversation piece for your friend's dinner table than for everyone who follows you on social media. Take the photos of your favorite haunts and make a genuine album rather than one on social media. That will prevent you from giving too much of yourself away and will help you re-engage with reality. Do not make yourself an easy target for a predator. Show them that you will not be made the victim and that your awareness of dark psychology tactics has equipped you to see them coming before they can do you harm.

# CHAPTER 8
*Deviant Behavior And Dark Psychology*

Dark psychology is a never-ending maze of nuances and terms, but it may be intriguing to you to know how dark psychology is a latent factor in a large number of criminal behaviors and labels. After all, the goal of most criminals is to achieve something for themselves by making a victim out of someone else. Few crimes are completely disconnected from other people and more often are committed because of how they affect other people. Once again, the dynamic of dark psychology is dependent on the relationship between the perpetrator and the victim. Notice that these terms have been used throughout this text but that they are also terms regularly used in law enforcement. That is not a coincidence. Dark psychology and criminality have a strong connection, and that is especially true of certain kinds of criminals.

## Criminal Labels

There are many kinds of criminal labels, such as robber or money launderer. These are not people we would want to encounter or people we would enjoy, but those labels do not spark the same level of fear as some others do. There is an implication behind each label that leads us to make judgments about what level of criminal someone could be. This is our own attempt to place them on the Dark Continuum in such a way that satisfies our understanding of others' depravity.

One criminal label that is commonly used is a **sociopath**. Do not confuse sociopaths with psychopaths. A psychopath has no conscience, lacks empathy, and acts on impulse. A sociopath, on the other hand, has a limited conscience and lacks empathy. Their limited conscience means they can fully understand if something is wrong and choose to do it anyway. It is also important to note that this is a clinical diagnosis and not something a layperson can use to describe a person without that official diagnosis. If you are unsure of which term may be appropriate, it is much better to avoid trying to label someone at all. It is tempting to describe someone you may know with such a strong diagnosis, but that is unfair to the individual and reduces the impact that these are a medical diagnosis and not simply titles created to describe certain people. These labels bear an immense wait and should not be taken lightly.

Sociopaths are almost harder to fathom than psychopaths because they do have a concept of what a conscience is. A true psychopath is not able to conceptualize right or wrong, so it is easier to see how they commit terrible crimes. A sociopath, however, is able to understand but goes through with their criminal acts anyway. They can almost seem like any other fully functioning human, except the fact that they can set aside morality and commit any number of crimes. They may know it is wrong, but they may not understand why it matters that it is wrong. Perhaps what is more important, then, is that they do not have the ability to empathize. If they cannot understand how their actions will cause someone pain or sadness or anger, etc., then you can begin to understand why they could move forward with their immoral act. They know it is wrong, but they do not see the consequences that the action will have on the victim emotionally. They are unable to rationalize how someone may react to the negative stimulus of something they do.

Sociopaths are also known to be antisocial. This does not mean that they avoid all social interactions, but rather that the interactions they do have, go against typical, acceptable behaviors when interacting with others. These individuals, when encountered in an everyday setting, would most likely stick out for all the wrong reasons. They will not be able to respond and emote in a way that makes sense to the observer. That is why the correct term for a sociopath is actually antisocial personality disorder (ASPD). The bottom line for a sociopath is that they cannot be motivated by the feelings of others, so the only natural motivator is their own desires. That means they will engage in any number of horrific acts because they have a disregard for societal norms and do not care about the emotional implications for others.

Sociopaths and psychopaths may have you thinking of serial killers, and you would not be wrong to do so. Serial killers are often diagnosed as suffering from mental illnesses that are ASPD or are associated with ASPD and psychopathy. You may recall that a serial killer has to have killed more than two people over a span of time. They are not like mass murderers who kill many in one large event or like a spree killer who kills multiple people over a shorter period of time. Serial killers can go through peaks and valleys throughout their killing careers and are often known to have "cooling off" periods that can last months or even years before they kill again.

A serial killer is most notable in dark psychology because of the extent to which they take their victimization. Dark psychology is about control, so, to a serial killer, the ultimate version of controlling a victim is murder. Once the victim is dead, the serial killer's control is complete. They may also enjoy the reactions of the victim because they lack empathy. In fact, the victim's reactions may provide them with a form of satisfaction or an emotional high that they cannot get in other circumstances.

Serial killers are also connected to narcissism and Machiavellianism. Serial killers would have a difficult time finding victims if they did not have the Dark Manipulation skills necessary to tempt victims to go with them or at least come near them. This is where Machiavellianism can come into play. The serial killer can fabricate carefully crafted lies that make the victim trust them or pity them. Then the victim's defenses are down, making it much easier for the serial killer to move forward with murdering them. Narcissism can be helpful for a serial killer because it can make them incredibly charming and self-assured. Confidence has its own kind of appeal, so a victim may find themselves believing in the trustworthiness of a serial killer wholeheartedly until it is too late. Both of these factors, as discussed before, can also be a downfall. Some notoriously narcissistic serial killers are so convinced of their own infallibility that they will try to represent themselves in court after they are caught. Their actual knowledge of the law plays no part in the decision because they are so convinced that they are too amazing to be outwitted by the justice system. They will adhere to the conviction that they are the best and deserve to be center stage, even if it means they risk being successfully prosecuted. This cockiness also means they can convince themselves that their lies are incredibly believable, but when someone comes along who is more self-aware, their lies can begin to unravel very quickly with a little careful scrutiny. That is why serial killers who are narcissists are often caught. The serial killers became so comfortable and predictable that it was only a matter of time before they were caught.

Another criminal label that can be difficult to understand but is still terrifying is an arsonist. An arsonist has a deep and abiding fascination with fire and the destruction it can cause., so they set fires to achieve an emotional high or some other kind of positive social return. They have a compulsion to set fires that can stem from any number of motivations or from seemingly no motivation at all.

We will first look at an arsonist who sets fires with a pre-existing motivation. These kinds of arsonists may be interested in revenge or may be interested in making themselves appear superior. They would fall on the Machiavellian corner of the Dark Triad. They have motives, they are methodical and thorough in their planning, and they will manipulate those around them to steer suspicion away from themselves. They also may be performative arsonists who are setting fires partially to gain information and partially to show off what they have done. They may even leave behind clues to taunt authorities or victims with the fact that they, the arsonist, have outwitted everyone else.

An arsonist who does not have a pre-existing motivation but who sets fires out of compulsion would more closely align with the psychopathic corner of the Dark Triad. There is a desire to act on impulse, to be chaotic, and to cause chaos. There is a complete disregard for consequences to others. They act with only the motivation to satisfy themselves and their need to create this chaos and destruction. In some ways, an arsonist resembles a sadist because they want to inflict a particular kind of pain, but they are often not directly motivated by hurting a particular victim.

Although arsonists have been included in this book, it is somewhat harder to make a case for how arsonists engage in dark psychology. There are victims of arson, yes, but the perpetrator is often less interested in the victims and more often fascinated by the fire and destruction of property. Whether or not people are victimized can be inconsequential. This is not always the case, and some arsonists do choose targets. However, they must be examined individually to determine whether or not dark psychology was a major, minor, or nonexistent contributor to the arsonist's actions. After all, an arsonist sets fires with the understanding that human victims may be involved. They understand this but set the fire anyway, so perhaps their victimization is that they do not care either way. If a fire creates a victim, that is of no consequence to the arsonist. The only goal is to start a fire.

Another criminal label that may stir some strong reactions is **terrorist**. A terrorist is someone who commits a violent or unlawful act that is designed to produce terror in the victims, often civilians, and is usually politically motivated. Terrorists are often aligned with an ideology that encourages them to engage in such acts frequently and with the design to create chaos and fear. These ideologies can have ties to governments, religions, or simply individuals who have created their own ideas around how the world should be. The acts of terror they commit are meant to cause a level of anarchy that will bring about the rise of their ideology and the fall of any opposing ideologies.

A terrorist has ties to dark psychology not so much because of what they do but because of why they do what they do. Behind most terrorists is an organization that is often headed by a leader. That terrorist leader is the key source of dark psychology. Similar to a cult leader, they will engage in any number of manipulation tactics to get their followers to perform terrorist acts. This includes brainwashing and mind games that are designed to break down the victim's previously held beliefs and coerce them into believing as the leader does. Then that victim becomes a new perpetrator. This means that the goal of the terrorist leader is to continually spawn new victims to become followers who then become perpetrators. This means that terrorist organizations may perhaps be more difficult to root out than some cults because the former victims who become perpetrators can learn to emulate the tactics used by their leaders and create mini-communities within the greater terrorist community. They replace their former susceptible personality with one that is manipulated into being by the leader. Once that transformation is complete, the victim has become a leader in their own way and is now free to perpetrate the same brainwashing and mind games on others in order to continue the cycle.

Terrorists can be closely aligned with psychopaths within the Dark Triad because they are invested in creating chaos, but the tactics they use are more Machiavellian in nature. The outcome is chaos and fear, but the plan was crafted methodically over time and was not an act of impulse. There is a dark design behind a terrorist organization. Otherwise, it would not be possible to continue to draw new members and turn them into new perpetrators. It is hard to say whether a terrorist can be said to lack empathy because they may be so brainwashed that they truly believe the crimes they commit are for the greater good. This does not and cannot excuse what they do, but it does beg the question of whether their free will was at play in the same way as someone who is not under the influence of a masterful Dark Manipulator. This also creates the conundrum of when or if the former victim, now perpetrator, has spent so long as a perpetrator that their previous role of victim becomes irrelevant. What is unclear is how to gauge when this line is crossed or whether the line exists at all. It is not clear cut, which is why terrorists are a difficult area of criminality to assess.

Another difficult criminal label to assess is a **sadist**. The sadist's goal is always the same, and that is to inflict some kind of pain or humiliation on someone else for the sake of satisfying the sadist's desires in some way. This falls squarely within the parameters of dark psychology. A sadist has no evolutionary motive for what they do. A sadist is always interested in victimizing. A sadist is also very interested in exacerbating and maximizing the dynamic between a victim and a perpetrator. They go beyond simply controlling the mind. They want their control to be so absolute that the victim's mind does not need to be controlled. The perpetrator has them so thoroughly within their power that they can inflict pain as they see fit. They manifest their control in an intense and readily apparent way. There is no question of whether the victim was exercising free will. The sadist's goal is to remove any kind of choice at all and leave the victim with only one option: pain.

It is important to note that a sadist differs from other kinds of deviant criminals because they are most interested in physical pain. Most other personality types and criminal types are also interested in psychological and emotional pain. A sadist will also enjoy this kind of pain, but the physical manifestation is definitely an important factor. What is also interesting about sadists is that they may be able to find willing victims. That sounds counterintuitive, but there are other kinds of people known as masochists who enjoy having pain inflicted on them. If a sadist is willing to take the time, they can seek out and find a masochist who will not only accept but enjoy the pain the sadist wants to inflict. Sometimes this scenario works out amicably, and both individuals are able to achieve the satisfaction they seek without there being any true victims. What they do is based on an agreement rather than coercion.

Sadists are most notable for the pleasure they derive from what they do. Watching others' pain is their pleasure, especially sexual pleasure. However, this means that many sadists will not be satisfied by inflicting pain on a masochist. Part of what gives them a thrill is the fact that their victim is not a willing participant in the pain. This is part of what increases their Dark Factor. They are disinterested in how others feel when pain is inflicted on them. The priority is the sadist's gratification at all times. This could be connected to egoism and/or narcissism. The sadist's needs and desires are the focal points, and the consequences to those around them are unimportant and trivial to the sadist. This is another label that many will find it hard to understand because they cannot understand why watching someone's fear, pain, and humiliation can create not just a sense of satisfaction but a sense of pleasure. This is not intended to shame those who engage in consensual acts with elements of sadism and/or masochism. Instead, it points to how a sadist's desire to inflict pain can take them further down the Dark Continuum and make it harder for others to understand their motivations and actions.

Another criminal label worth exploring is the **necrophile**. This is another label that is difficult to fathom as an average human being. A necrophile is someone who is attracted to corpses in a sexual way. This does not necessarily mean that these individuals intend to or have intercourse with corpses but rather that they are drawn to them and find the fact that they are dead sexually satisfying or arousing. There may also be some kind of spectrum within necrophilia because some individuals may be satisfied with the illusion that their victim is dead. This could be created by a drug-induced state or by some kind of role-playing scenario. There does not necessarily have to be a truly dead body for the necrophile to find gratification and enjoyment.

Now to examine how necrophilia may fit into the boundaries of dark psychology. Although a corpse is already dead, the argument could be made that a corpse is an ideal victim because they have no means to resist whatever acts are inflicted upon them by the necrophile. It is also an ideal setup for the perpetrator to have complete control over the victim in every way. However, necrophilia creates a very difficult situation when trying to analyze it from a dark psychological perspective. Although there is a perpetrator and there is a victim, the complication arises that the victim is dead. This means there is no mind to control nor actions to coerce. The other human being that the perpetrator is meant to have controlled is essentially no longer a human being once they are deceased. This begets the question of whether necrophiles should be considered a part of the Dark Continuum at all.

The undeniable connection between necrophilia and dark psychology is that it is often the case that the necrophile murdered the person that then becomes the corpse they are sexually attracted to. This is a definite example of extreme control and victimization. The perpetrator is so intent on reaching sexual gratification that they will use their control over the victim to first murder the victim and turn them into an attractive corpse. This is a very Machiavellian tendency because the manipulator is highly focused on one goal and will use any means to reach that goal.

The list of criminal labels could go on, but this is enough exposure to show you how dark psychology helps to illuminate what can make these criminals so successful in perpetrating their crimes. The power of the Dark Triad is undeniable, so when individuals engage in deviant behavior and also show dark personality traits, it is no wonder they become dangerous and often violent criminals. The narcissist, Machiavellian, and psychopath can all be at work alongside these other deviant criminal tendencies, which creates a Dark Factor that is incredibly strong. These Dark Manipulators can go to new and unknown places on the Dark Continuum, and it is possible that someday one of them will show us the true meaning of the Dark Singularity.

# CHAPTER 9
*Making Dark Psychology Work For You*

You have finally made it nearly to the end of your journey into dark psychology and its many nuances. You will now have a thorough understanding of what it means to engage in dark psychology tactics and how the people around you may be using dark psychology to control and manipulate you. However, what is missing is how you can use dark psychology. After all, you are human, and every human has the capacity to engage in dark psychology. What this chapter aims to teach you is how you can take certain tactics and use them to create desirable outcomes for both you and the victim. This advice is not intended to encourage you to victimize others but rather to understand how dark psychology tactics can positively influence your life and do nothing negative to the "victim." In these scenarios, the "victim" is not being hurt by what you are doing. They may be giving you what you want because you used dark manipulation, but they will not be victimized by whatever you get out of the situation.

This section is not exhaustive, and it is always possible to go back through the text and discover another tactic you can reinvent to create positive effects. What you need to keep front of mind is that what you do is always done to induce good. As with the chapter on social media, question yourself about your motivations. Who does this benefit the most? What will be its short-term and long-term effects? Why do I want to do this? Will this encourage more positive developments for everyone involved? Will I be lying if I engage in this behavior? Each of these answers will let you see for yourself if you are straying too far down the Dark Continuum. That is the whole purpose of this book. The goal is to give you the power to understand yourself and those around you on a new level. You can now understand if your motivations are coming from a desire to do good or from a deeply human but possibly dark place within you where truly dark psychology lurks.

## Revisiting Some Dark Tactics

In order to put you well on your way to practicing dark psychology, it is best to simply revisit some of the tactics discussed earlier, but this time to show how you can use those tactics to create positive outcomes for everyone involved. This may sound impossible or like it is a trap. That is not the point of these tips and tricks. They are meant to show how the victim can strike back and how the psychological and emotional push of dark psychology tactics can actually make the "victims" more fulfilled also. There is a way to lie on the lighter end of the Dark Continuum while still using dark psychology on a regular basis.

## Choice Restriction

As you may recall from the chapter that explains some key terms, choice restriction is when a perpetrator provides a victim with choices but intentionally omits any choices the perpetrator finds undesirable. This is controlling because the victim is not a part of creating the choices and is duped into thinking they had a choice because multiple options were presented. It can be very misleading.

When you use choice restriction, what you are doing is limiting the "victim's" choices in such a way that helps the "victim" avoid making a mistake that may negatively impact both of your lives. For example, the "victim" could be your best friend who is deciding how to break up with an abusive partner and is now uncertain whether they want to break it off at all. As the perpetrator, you could tell them that they only have three choices, and within those three choices, you would only include scenarios that ended in the "victim" breaking up with their abusive partner. This is a positive way to use choice restriction because you are most interested in helping the "victim" rather than making them act in a way that is most beneficial to yourself.

## Gift Giving

Gift giving can be manipulative when the gift giver's goal is to use the recipient's guilt to coerce them into doing a favor or returning the favor in a way that most benefits the giver. The perpetrator will often make the gift something large or very thoughtful in order to increase the likelihood that the victim will agree to do whatever the perpetrator desires.

When using gift giving positively, you are still going to give a gift that is thoughtful or large. This will still induce a sense of guilt in the "victim," but the goal or motivator should be to push the victim in a positive direction. For example, imagine that a family member has been neglecting to call and check on you even though you have recently fallen on hard times. In the past, you have always been there for them in similar situations and never failed to support them and check on them regularly. Rather than call them out for being neglectful, you can use the gift to remind them how hard you work to have a positive relationship with them, and this may push the "victim" to feel guilty enough to realize they have neglected you recently. This can save you an awkward conversation, and it can also help the "victim" regain some clarity about your relationship.

## Guilt Inducement

Guilt inducement is similar in many ways to gift giving, except that it uses words instead of gifts to push the victim into taking action. Guilt inducement is the intentional use of statements or other behaviors to make a victim feel guilty for not being better to the perpetrator. These comments are often done passive-aggressively but are blatantly designed to make the victim feel such immense guilt that they may do any number of things to make the perpetrator feel better.

Guilt inducement can be an effective tool for positive change when used very carefully. Positive guilt inducement is best created through actions rather than through words because the "victim" may pick up on the passive-aggressive comments too easily. For example, imagine you have a sloppy roommate who was supposed to have cleared out the laundry room for you but instead has left their clothes strewn about and still in the dryer. Then, if the roommate asks you to go somewhere to some event, you can tell them you cannot. When the roommate asks you "why," you can respond that you have to wait until your clothes are washed because you do not have anything clean and appropriate to wear. You cannot, of course, make this comment sarcastically but, instead, have to show how sincerely sorry you are that you cannot make it. This should coerce the "victim" into realizing they were the reason you had to say no. It should also coerce them into finishing their chore so you can enjoy whatever event they wanted to attend. This creates positive outcomes for everyone.

Love Denial

Love denial is meant to make the victim miss the perpetrator's affection so much that they will do nearly anything to restore the perpetrator's displays of affection. This could mean the perpetrator does not touch the victim or refuses to participate in other outward shows of affection.

Love denial can be an effective tool in a relationship. This has to be a tactic that is not used frequently, and it must always be explained directly to the victim. For example, you could have a partner who has trouble listening to you when you have something truly serious to say to them. Perhaps you have already brought this topic several times before, but your partner still has not shown they recognize what you are trying to communicate. The next time the issue arises, you could begin using love denial. When your partner asks what is wrong, you then explain that you cannot show them affection until they show you an equal measure of affection by listening to what you have to communicate. They should be willing to take what you say more seriously when the stakes are so high. It is also an effective way to get your partner to pay attention when they may have become complacent in your relationship.

Love Flooding

Love flooding is the act of overwhelming someone with love and affection. It can be used to create a false sense of commitment and caring in a relationship. It can also lure a victim into believing that they are extremely important to the perpetrator, when, in fact, the perpetrator is only interested in how they can coerce the victim to behave as they desire. It is also a misleading title because excessive compliments and other displays of affection do not necessarily equate to love.

Love flooding can be a positive choice in a relationship if your partner is perhaps becoming so comfortable in the relationship that they stop trying to show you how important you are to them. If you then flood them with love, you can remind them that your relationship goes beyond the trivial and is something special and separate from a mere friendship. Remind them through your love flooding that you cherish them and that your relationship is something that drives how you live your daily life. It is a chance for your partner to feel valued and appreciated again. This should be enough to shake them out of their stupor and guide them back to showering you with love and affection also. It can be a great way to rebook a relationship for both partners.

### Priming

Priming is very subtle, and it may be a difficult skill to develop. Priming is the use of specific words or phrases along with related actions that encourage a person to have a particular response. These are subtle suggestions that get you primed to behave a certain way or have a certain response to a situation. You could think of priming as similar to grooming. Habits of thought are developed through carefully planted priming tactics.

Priming can be an excellent way to get someone to have a positive reaction to a request. For example, imagine you have a new project you want to present to your boss that really has the potential to make a large and lasting impact on the business. Rather than say that outright, you could prime your boss to have a positive response to your idea by dropping subtle hints about it in the weeks leading up to your presentation. Make little side comments on related topics or share a desirable development that would improve the company. When the boss hears your presentation, these subtle thoughts will creep back into their conscience and encourage them to hear your presentation with enthusiasm and encouragement. They may even feel like this is the idea they have been waiting for because your subtle hints all clearly led to this one central idea.

### Reverse Psychology

Reverse psychology is an old tactic that you may already have used or have heard about so many times that you doubt its effectiveness. However, reverse psychology can still have a significant impact on someone's behavior. It is the conscious decision to encourage someone to act in a certain way that actually makes them do the opposite. That is the intent of the perpetrator all along. This is most effective when the victim is trying to strike back at the perpetrator in some way. They will do the opposite of what the perpetrator says out of a desire to deny them what they want.

Reverse psychology can have a positive effect when used carefully and in carefully chosen situations. For example, imagine that you have a friend who is angry at you for standing up to them when they treated a mutual friend poorly. What you could tell them is maybe they should just give up on your friendship if they want to act this way. The friend may respond that that is a good idea and act like they are going to leave you and end your friendship. What happens instead is that they will be so angry and so intent on not giving you what you want that they will begin arguing for your friendship and why you should stay friends. Now they are fighting for you to work through your differences rather than to allow the friendship to go through a falling out.

Withdrawal

Withdrawal can be a very dangerous action to take because it can so easily coerce a victim into inviting a perpetrator back into their lives because they "miss" them so much. It can be intensely manipulative because the victim will feel deprived of the perceived benefits they enjoyed while the perpetrator was still there.

Withdrawal can be an effective tool when a "victim" needs to see what the "perpetrator" is bringing to their relationship and relearn to appreciate the benefits of the relationship. Imagine you are in a romantic relationship, and your partner has begun to be obsessed with their career to the point that your relationship is always on hold because work comes first. However, your partner is still enjoying the benefits of your affection and attention without reciprocating. What you can do is first and foremost let them know you are withdrawing and why. Simply explain that you have noticed that they seem to need more time for their work and less time with you. You can present it as a way to help them get what they want. If they truly want to be dedicated so fully to work, then removing yourself from the picture should bring the "victim" closer to their desires. What it will do instead is show the "victim" how the "perpetrator" has been giving far more than they are receiving. This will encourage the "victim" to do what it takes to restore balance in the relationship so that both participants are actively engaged in developing together.

**Leading Questions**

Leading questions are designed to be a trap. The perpetrator will ask questions to which the victim has to respond yes. This allows the perpetrator to create a standard of response or behavior to which the victim must adhere in order to be consistent and stand by what they said. This is a common tactic among fundraisers. They will ask if you agree with a series of statements, perhaps about your commitment to helping the poor, and if you respond yes to every question, then it would seem unfeeling or contradictory to refuse to donate to a project that serves the very ideals you just verbally supported.

Leading questions can be a highly effective tool when you want to help guide someone to a logical conclusion without telling them directly what to do. For example, you may have a friend who is contemplating a career change from something more lucrative to something that is less lucrative but more fulfilling. You can ask a series of leading questions that help them see how feeling fulfilled is more important to them than money. This helps guide them to a decision that is more beneficial to them than it is to you.

Whether you choose to employ these tactics or not is your choice. Your study of dark psychology does not require that you practice dark psychology. These tactics are meant to give you a framework that will enable you to manipulate and coerce great things for yourself and, more importantly, for the people you care about. That is what will separate you from the other practitioners of dark psychology and keep you away from some of the darker topics we have covered in this book. Always ground your choices in a desire to do good for all rather than only to benefit yourself, and you will find yourself living in the light rather than the darkness.

As you revisit this toolkit, challenge yourself to look for new ways to make dark psychology work for you. You already have it in you, so why not use it to make your life better. Take control of your life back. Understand who and what is controlling your life now and how you lost control in the first place. Dark psychology can give you back what you lost and give you the confidence to step out into the world, knowing you are well-equipped to avoid being the victim.

# CONCLUSION

Thank you for making it through to the end of *Dark Psychology Secrets*. The hope is that it gave you an understanding of the darkness that can infiltrate your life and seek to make you a victim. It is also meant to guide you to recognize those around you who may be using dark psychology to influence your life.

You first learned how to define dark psychology and understand its role in humanity. You then were able to explore the basic defining qualities of dark psychology, like the Dark Triad. After that, you learned an extensive number of terms that not only relate to dark psychology but also relate to other fields of study.

You now know what tactics are used by those who embrace dark psychology. You have the knowledge to see these tactics at work and to extricate yourself from their potentially negative influences. You also know who is more likely to engage in dark psychology simply by assessing their career choices and current occupation.

You are well-aware of how dark psychology can dig into the depths of evil in the form of deviant behavior and extremely dark individuals who have strayed closer and closer to the Dark Singularity. You can see how dark influences may lurk online when you open your social media accounts each day. You may have a fresh perspective on a famous criminal and how dark psychology changed the course of their criminal careers.

The next step is to take what you have learned and put it to use. You can now share it with others and help them discover how to avoid being the target of victimization. The point is that the choice is yours, and therefore the power is yours.

Finally, if you found this book useful in any way, be sure to leave a review on Amazon or recommend it to a friend.

# DESCRIPTION

Have you ever wondered why you let yourself be guided and influenced by people you know are not good? Have you ever wanted to know how to avoid toxic relationships and manipulative people? Have you ever contemplated why certain people act the way they do? Have you ever felt your skin crawl because you knew someone was up to something, but you couldn't say what?

All of these questions can be answered with a quick study of the secrets of dark psychology. You no longer have to live in fear or doubt but will instead be equipped with all the tools you need to detect and deter dark forces that surround you on a daily basis. You will also begin to see how the darkness is all around you but is also avoidable. Your knowledge will expand in new and exciting ways as you dive deeper into dark psychology. In this book, you will discover:

- What dark psychology is
- The history behind the development of dark psychology as a field of study
- The characteristics that make dark psychology unique and also a menacing force
- The many complex terms associated with dark psychology and what they mean
- The methodology of dark psychology and how its tools can be used to terrible effect
- Who is most likely to use dark psychology and why
- Who has gone the deepest into the darkness and why
- How social media can be a powerful platform for practitioners of dark psychology
- The ways in which deviant behavior can be traced back to roots in dark psychology
- How to put dark psychology to use in your own life

All of this and more awaits you in *Dark Psychology Secrets*. It is an in-depth look at this field of study intended to make you an expert who is empowered and savvy.

Once you have read this book, you will be able to see the world from a totally new perspective. Each time you interact with someone, you will have a new sense of how their motivations could be influencing their actions. You will also have the power to see through their lies and tactics before you become their latest victim.

This book is also full of some of the important terms that are relevant to the study of this field. Instead of feeling inept or uninformed, you will become an authority on dark psychology. You will find others turning to you for guidance and information.

*Dark Psychology Secrets* is also for the curious who want to know more about the darker side of humanity. People are capable of horrific deeds, and dark psychology is the key to understanding how and why someone can engage in such monstrous acts. The possibilities are endless, and those who seek will find the answers in this book.

Finally, this text is the answer to how you prevent others from taking advantage of you. You will never again be steered by others but will rest easy knowing you have control of your own choices.

www.ingramcontent.com/pod-product-compliance
Lightning Source LLC
Chambersburg PA
CBHW071455070526
44578CB00001B/344